A New Beginning

David Torkington has sold over 400,000 books and been translated into 13 languages.

BOOKS BY DAVID TORKINGTON

The Primacy of Loving – The Spirituality of the Heart

Wisdom from The Christian Mystics – How to Pray the Christian Way

Wisdom from the Western Isles – The Making of a Mystic

Wisdom from Franciscan Italy – The Primacy of Love

How to Pray – A Practical Guide to the Spiritual Life

Prayer Made Simple – CTS booklet

Inner Life – A Fellow Traveller's Guide to Prayer

A New Beginning – A Sideways Look at the Spiritual Life

Dear Susanna – It's Time for a Christian Renaissance Passport to Perfection

Never Too Late to Love – Our Lady's Sublime Teaching on Prayer

His website is https://www.davidtorkington.com

A New Beginning

A Sideways Look at the Spiritual Life

DAVID TORKINGTON

MERCIER PRESS

Mercier Press, 82c Ballyhooly Road, St. Luke's, Cork, Ireland

First Published by Darton, Longman & Todd Ltd., London, 2024
This Edition Published by Mercier Press, 2025
Copyright © David Torkington, 2024

The moral rights of David Torkington to be identified as the author of this work have been asserted in accordance with the Copyright and Related Rights Act, 2000.

All rights reserved. This book is copyright material and must not be copied, reproduced, transferred, distributed, leased, licensed or publicly performed or used in any way except as specifically permitted in writing by the publisher, as allowed under the terms and conditions under which it was purchased or as strictly permitted by applicable copyright law. Any unauthorised distribution or use of this text may be a direct infringement of the author's and publisher's rights, and those responsible may be liable in law accordingly.

Ebook ISBN: 9781917453714
Original Edition ISBN: 9781917453455
Hardcover ISBN: 9781806900305
Large Print ISBN: 9781806900350
Cover design by The Sisters at the Benedictines of Mary, Queen of Apostles

Contents

Introduction	15
Chapter 1 – Could have tried harder	21
Chapter 2 – My left foot	26
Chapter 3 – Stop striving, start sliding	32
Chapter 4 – There's not a lot of it about	37
Chapter 5 – Mr Fix-it	42
Chapter 6 – The best of all possible starts	48
Chapter 7 – With thanks to Jumbo Jackson	54
Chapter 8 – Know thyself	60

Chapter 9 – Instructions not included — 65

Chapter 10 – Mac and the art of motor car maintenance — 70

Chapter 11 – A man in a million — 76

Chapter 12 – The call to pregnancy — 82

Chapter 13 – Famous for fifteen minutes — 87

Chapter 14 – The sixty-four-thousand-dollar question — 93

Chapter 15 – The art of the impossible — 98

Chapter 16 – The man with no arms or legs — 103

Chapter 17 – Dead men tell no lies — 108

Chapter 18 – Henry the confessor — 114

Chapter 19 – It's only a wave of a wand away	120
Chapter 20 – Where time touched eternity	126
Chapter 21 – Pride and prejudice	133
Chapter 22 – The Agony and the Ecstasy	139
Chapter 23 – A perpendicular paradise	145
Chapter 24 – In an English country garden	150
Chapter 25 – The two in one	156
Chapter 26 – No need to be alarmed	162
Chapter 27 – The cradle of contemplation	168
Chapter 28 – Three-legged love	174

Chapter 29 – The sacrament of touch	180
Chapter 30 – The frog prince	185
Chapter 31 – There is no substitute for experience	190
Chapter 32 – If at first you don't succeed	196
Chapter 33 – Practice makes perfect	201
Chapter 34 – Up with the violin, down with the kneeler	206
Chapter 35 – In vino veritas	212
Chapter 36 – Monastic medicine	217
Chapter 37 – Mr Swingtime's special	223
Chapter 38 – From Siberia with love	228
Chapter 39 – Mary's Sacrifice	234

Chapter 40 – A time to mourn,
a time to cry   239

Chapter 41 – Seize the moment   245

Chapter 42 – Living in the
Present Moment   250

Chapter 43 – Hacking into heaven   256

Chapter 44 – Hobson's choice?   261

Chapter 45 – The Alien Corn   267

Chapter 46 – St David of Didsbury   273

Chapter 47 – A very unlikely superstar   278

Chapter 48 – If only the canon hadn't
gone off   283

Chapter 49 – What we want
is more prisms!   289

CHAPTER 50 – BACK TO THE FUTURE   294

CHAPTER 51 – A DROP IN THE OCEAN   300

CHAPTER 52 – A NEW BEGINNING   305

Introduction

For the first Christians the Sun became a symbol of the endless and ever-flowing love of the infinite God that poured and continues to pour out of our Risen Lord. Prayer is the word used by Catholic tradition to describe what we must do over a whole lifetime to receive this love into our lives. My book, A New Beginning - A Sideways Look at the Spiritual Life, is a simple step by step guide that details what we must do in our prayer life to receive this love. I have tried to write it with the spoonfulls of sugar that help the medicine go down!

This profound spiritual journey must be made in the context of a whole religious way of daily life, of living, thinking and of behaving that makes this possible, hence this book A New Beginning. This way of life is called a Spirituality because it is totally orientated towards receiving God's infinite love that continually pours out of our Risen Lord. This loving that has united the Three in One in infinite loving from eternity, is not a thing but a divine person called the Holy Spirit. That is why the whole gamut of a Christian life that is created in order to receive his infinite loving is called a Spirituality, more specifically a Christian Spirituality. This book A New Beginning that is a companion to Inner Life - A Fellow Traveller's Guide to Prayer, is its indispensable twin. They are both most effective when read together, or at least one is read immediately after the other.

My recent release Never too Late to Love shows the indispensable importance of Our Lady's prayer, inspiration and guidance in early Christian Spirituality. It shows how she taught the Apostles and then the first Christians by her own example both in Jerusalem and her final home near Ephesus with her new son, St John. It was Jesus himself who gave him to her for their mutual spiritual and material wellbeing just before he died. She taught them continually before her Assumption into heaven, by both word and example, where and how this sublime spiritual journey finds its completion and how her prayer can support us along The Way.

For over sixty five years I have been studying and trying to live the most ancient and hallowed Catholic traditional teaching on spirituality and prayer that began after the sending of the Holy Spirit on the first Pentecost day. I have therefore, hopefully, been able to express and detail the God-given spirituality that Our Lord introduced into the early Church in a unique way. I have tried to do this by using plain simple contemporary English, employing modern metaphors, similes, examples and stories, as Our Lord did in his day. I have done this while adding to that spirituality the legitimate and approved practices of later saints and mystics. It is from them too, that we can learn to enter ever more deeply into the mystical life and loving of our Risen Lord.

Like its twin Inner Life, this book, A new Beginning, was not republished by its previous publishers. Although it sold 2,000 copies almost immediately they thought that as nobody had heard of me before, except my readers in the Catholic Herald, it would not be advisable to reprint another 2,000 books. Instead they asked me to write another book called Dear Susanna which went on to sell another 2,000 copies. This, 'quick print and bury them' approach to publishing which is the last refuge of visionless publishers is understandable, but it does close all possibility of producing the best sellers that are the making and the securing of all publishers. Within a few years my publishers went bust!

As the name of the new publishing house Essentialist Press suggests, they have committed themselves to publish only those books that go to the very essence of serious contemporary issues that are in the forefront of modern readers' minds. Seeing that the Catholic Church is busily employed in planning its own downfall and destruction by introducing modern heresies and trying to pass them off as part of a new orthodoxy, Essentialist Press has decided to act. They have decided to act to reassert true theological orthodoxy, and to promote traditional teaching on prayer and the spiritual life that is the only antidote to this modern madness. I am delighted to have been asked to support them in this task with my latest and future books and video podcasts.

My books that have been written to do precisely what is their present objective, will be accompanied by a course that takes the form of free visual podcasts on prayer that should be well underway by the time this book is published. The way ahead within the Catholic Church may seem bleak just now but remember that Our Lady of Fatima has promised that her Immaculate Heart, her gift to the Church in these terrible times, will ultimately prevail. If you are prepared to set out now on A New beginning and without delay, for we are indeed in the last minute of extra time, then please be reassured by the words of St Padre Pio, "Pray trust and don't worry".

Chapter 1

Could have tried harder

Every year at school was an annus horribilis for me because I did not exactly excel in the academic field, so I put all my energies into excelling on the playing field. If every year was an annus horribilis then there were three particular days that were a dies horribilis, days which I dreaded more than any others. These were the days when my school report arrived. Fortunately my father usually missed the morning post, so I had the whole day to think of ways and means of avoiding him that evening.

If I could not go out I would try hiding upstairs where he would not find me. But one way or the other the time would inevitably come when I would hear his voice resounding up the stairs. "David, where are you, where are you?" It reminded me of the voice of God calling out to Adam who had fled, like me, because he was ashamed of what he did, or in my case what I did not do. I know I should have had the courage to face up to my failures, and to my father too, as soon as possible and get it all over with, but I never did.

Unfortunately I fell into the bad habit of running away from my failures. That is why my weekly confession became a fortnightly confession, and then monthly, and then it took me all the courage I could muster to make it at Easter or thereabouts. All this was in the early fifties when boys like me were so innocent that they did not really think of their parents or teachers, let alone their priests, as sinners. I remember being shocked when I heard that every priest had to go to confession. Then I read St John's famous letter when he said that we are all sinners, and if we say we are not then we are deceiving ourselves and calling God a liar. It was quite an eyeopener for me.

I was in the sixth form before I found out that the saints were sinners too; at least that is how they started out, and some of them had been ten times the sinner I was, something I found hard to believe until a retreat master gave us a few examples that started me thinking. I thought about it so much that I put a question in the box provided for question time at the end of the retreat.

That retreat was given by Father Bassett SJ and it was one of the best I have ever attended. He told us that only Mary was immaculately conceived and that meant the rest of us were not. We were all born sinners and born into a sinful world. The difference between the saints and us is not that they did not sin and we do. The difference is that they had the humility to accept their sinfullness and their sins whenever they committed them. They did not run away and hide with shame as we do. They had the courage to admit what they had done immediately and sought forgiveness from the One they had offended.

Fr Bassett gave St Peter as an example. The moment Peter betrayed Jesus he was sorry and sought forgiveness without delay. We were given many more examples from the life of St Peter and other saints to show that the real difference between them and us was not sin but the swiftness with which they faced up to the sins they committed and the forgiveness they needed. I was relieved that I was not the only one to run away from my shame and put off the forgiveness I needed—even the saints did it. But they finally became what God wants us to become by the ever-increasing urgency with which they turned back to him after they had fallen. Fr Bassett's talk on the presence of

God was a great help because it made me realise that God knows exactly what we have done and pursues us until we admit it, as he did with Adam in the garden.

God is always there, searching us out, and he is always saying, "Where are you?", not because he does not know where we are, but because we do not know where we are, nor where we are going when sin and shame make us run from the only One who can heal us.

The first measure of genuine progress in the spiritual life is not the absence of sin, but the time it takes from the sin we inevitably fall into to the moment when we have the humility to ask for the forgiveness we need and the grace to begin again. I am still trying to shorten that time, so that when my final report is read out from the rooftops at least it will say, "He tried", even if it goes on to say, "He could have tried harder."

Chapter 2

My left foot

I damaged my foot. I cannot be more specific than that because I did not have the courage to go to my doctor. The last time I saw him he said, "And if you insist on wearing sandals like that you'll do permanent damage to your feet." The next day I missed the bus and had to walk home in the condemned sandals, and that did it.

As I lay in bed that night, tossing and turning, I could hear my mother's voice echoing from the past, "He won't be told, he simply won't be told." As I did not have the courage to go back to the doctor I had to play nurse to myself. To begin with I sank into deep self-pity and probably would have remained there had it not been market day. But I simply had to get my fresh fruit and veg, especially if I could not get any exercise, so I dragged myself up and hobbled to the bus stop.

The whole day turned out to be a 'liberating experience' as one of my friends put it after his first therapy session. But let me explain what I mean. After I did the market, I did the supermarket and then the hypermarket and I did it as I have never done it before – with the greatest pleasure.

Once I faced the fact that I could only move at half the knots I made before, I sailed round with good grace, as if propelled by a gentle breeze instead of the explosive engine that drove me round before. I knocked no one over, I did not even shoulder anyone out of my way, and I waited for ten minutes at the supermarket checkout with the patience of Job. I actually smiled at the cashier when her receipt roll ran out and we had to wait for the supervisor who had gone for her elevenses.

The cashier told me all about her cruise in the Mediterranean from Genoa to Venice. We did every port of call in Italy and one in Corsica before the supervisor turned up - and I did not mind at all. I would have blown at least four cylinders on any other day, and a couple of gaskets too, but on that day I simply did not mind at all. I just sailed on regardless to the hypermarket, with all the time in the world to nod at acquaintances and chat with fair-weather friends whom I would not normally have noticed as I stormed around the shops on the worst day of the week - market day.

It not only turned out to be the best day of the week, but that week turned out to be the best week of the year because I had more time, more quality time, than I could ever remember before. I found that the old cliché, 'more haste less speed' is really true. I did not do any less that week than when my foot was enjoying the same health as the rest of my body, and in one very important way I did more.

Previously was so lost in me and mine that I had no time for them and theirs. But now, nodding acquaintances were becoming fair-weather friends, and fair-weather friends were becoming all-weather friends, while old weather-worn friends suddenly received letters and phone calls they had not had for years.

I got further that week than I had for months, at least in what really matters. When you stop long enough to think about it, what on earth matters more than relationships, or in heaven for that matter? The older I get the more I come to realise and appreciate that there is nothing more important than relationships. After all that is where the word 'religion' came from in the first place, because that is what religion is all about. In the end it may well be more about our relationship with God than any other, but in the beginning it is more about our relationships with others.

That is why St John pointed out that you cannot love the God you are unable to see until you can love the brother you can see. If a retreat is supposed to be a time for slowing down, for taking stock and for reviewing the way one's life is going, my damaged foot gave me the retreat I have been in need of for far too long. It is almost better now so there was not anything seriously wrong, but there was something seriously wrong with the way my life was going. It was going far too fast for my own good and the good of my friends too.

I have not thrown the sandals away yet. They are left by the front door to remind me on the way out to slow down, to stop dashing around like there is no tomorrow, because if not, there will be no today – no today that is worth living anyway.

Who wants to live any day without friends? I know that I do not even want to live without fair-weather friends, or even nodding acquaintances for that matter. I wouldd rather have a damaged foot any day, wouldn't you?

Chapter 3

Stop striving, start sliding

I had just bought myself a new jacket in a clothing store and was halfway down the escalator when I realised I had left my credit card with the assistant. On impulse I turned and began to run up the moving staircase, only to find I was forced to stop to catch my breath a metre or two before I reached the top. By the time I recovered sufficiently to start again I was more than halfway to the bottom. I tried again and again before I finally threw in the towel and used the lift.

The shock of experiencing the decline of my physical powers was compounded by the shock of experiencing the decline in my mental powers when the assistant correctly assured me that I had put the card into my breast pocket. However, the whole incident turned out to be what my driving instructor would have called a 'learning experience'. The moment you stop going forwards is the moment when you start going backwards. You cannot stand still on the spiritual journey. No matter whether you are a beginner or whether you have been travelling for half a lifetime or more, the moment you stop striving is the moment when you start sliding.

I remember reading an old-fashioned meditation book when I was in my first enthusiasm that told the story of a young novice who was so lost in prayer that he rose from the choir stalls and kissed the feet of Our Lady's statue that stood by the cross on the rood screen. But when he died he descended into the very depths of hell where he burned for eternity for the lust that led him to leave the monastery to which he was called. Of course, like so many stories common to that particular literary genre it was way over the top, but the point it wanted to make was, and still is, valid. It does not matter to what height you may rise in the spiritual ascent, the moment you stop striving is the moment you start sliding, and if you do nothing to stop yourself, you will end up in a far worse state than when you started.

We used to have a special prize at school donated by the Bishop and presented on speech day to the boy in each class who had tried his best. I remember the headmaster saying in his address to the parents that he considered it to be the most important of all the prizes, because nothing mattered more than how well a person tried. I never won that prize, but I have never forgotten those words and I found them echoed in later life when I read Simone Weil, the French Jewish philosopher who said that "We are no more than the quality of our endeavour". That more than anything defines what a person is before God, or before anyone else for that matter. As long as we are trying we are going forward, but the moment we stop trying is the moment when we start going backwards, like that middle-aged man on the escalator.

Nevertheless, all the trying in the world put together and multiplied by ten would not get anyone anywhere had Someone not succeeded. It is his success that we celebrate at Easter. He arrived at where we all want to go because he never stopped trying to open himself to the love that finally raised him into the fullness of life that he came to give everyone who is ready to receive it. That is the life that overflowed from him on the first Pentecost day and onto and into all who continually try to receive it.

Perhaps the profoundest of all proverbs is, "God helps those who help themselves". The trouble is, like so many proverbs it has become a cliché and nobody values it anymore. Yet this cliché sums up so simply one of the most profound and complex truths of the spiritual life. Tome after theological tome has been written in an attempt to explain the mystery of what God does and what we have to do to cooperate with him as the spiritual life unfolds. But that little cliché tells us all we practically need to know for the journey ahead. The only mistake we can make is to stop trying, or to try too hard. Trying too hard always means failure because it is the expression of an arrogant self-belief that makes a person act as if everything depended on themselves and not on God. "If you must try, try gently", as Oliver Hardy said to Stan Laurel.

The consistent but gentle way in which we try daily to journey on in the spiritual life not only reveals an inner humility of heart that knows that without God we can do nothing, but at the same time keeps that heart open at all times to receive the grace he never refuses.

Chapter 4

There's not a lot of it about

It all began with a pain in my stomach that woke me up in the middle of the night and kept me awake for hours. When my temperature rose and my sore throat ploughed its way into the back of my mouth I went to see my doctor, who told me, "There's a lot of it about." He told me to go to bed, take plenty of liquid, two aspirins every six hours and not to bother him again, because 'there was a lot of it about'.

I stopped at a supermarket on the way home to take in provisions for the duration. There were not many people there, because 'there was a lot of it about', so the cashier was able to give me more time than my doctor did. She told me it was not really flu, it was just the usual seasonal cold that she had for weeks, but she never missed a day, unlike the wimps with whom she worked who all took to their beds.

She seemed far better informed than my doctor and prescribed a cold remedy or a hot toddy made with the whisky that they had on special offer. I tried that whisky before so I bought the cold remedy instead. It was rather more expensive but had a far better taste and it guarantees you sleep through the night instead of waking up sweating with the inevitable headache.

I spent almost four days in bed and was so ill that I could not even get up for the last episode of an Agatha Christie mystery on the television. I am over the worst of it now but I felt so exhausted that I had to sit down for half an hour after brushing my teeth. Everything left me flat. I know I am always writing about the spiritual life, but it has not meant much to me for the last week or more and I cannot pretend I have done much praying either.

Of course I've been depressed. Who would not feel depressed when all drive and energy leaves you and you feel no enthusiasm for anything at all and full of negative thoughts. They have made me want to rip up my latest typescript on prayer telling other people how to do what I have not been able to do myself. I know what will happen the moment I feel well again – I will be full of guilt for missing yet another wonderful opportunity to practise patience in adversity.

I know that even the most perfunctory of prayers when you are in the pits is worth ten times the prayer that flows so fluently when feeling on top of the world. I know that the most powerful prayer that was ever prayed was made amid terrible suffering and inner darkness by the man I admire more than any other. But translating admiration into imitation has always exposed the gap between the person I am and the person I ought to be. If you want to know the quality of your inner life then look no further than how you behave when sickness has left you feeling down and depressed. If you discover that when you have been weighed in this balance, you have been found wanting, do not give up. Make a resolution with me to try better next time round. I know I have made these resolutions before and I know I will make them again, but the genuine desire to try again despite past failures is all important. When that goes everything goes.

Unlike any other judge, God will judge us not by what we have achieved but by how much we have tried, by the quality of our endeavour and by the serious way in which we resolve to try again no matter how many times we may have failed. Only a spiritual ignoramus would say that the road to hell is paved with good intentions. If they are genuinely good intentions they will inevitably lead to another place and to the Person we desire more than any other.

So next time sickness brings you low and makes you feel that you are unable to pray from the heart or even say any prayers, try to offer up the matchwood cross that you have to bear alongside the cross that Christ had to bear. If you can do that for at least some of the time it might enable you to unite yourself with the most potent and powerful prayer that has ever been made, and to experience, albeit in a small and distant way, what it cost to make it. That is real prayer and 'there is not a lot of it about'.—would that there was.

Chapter 5

Mr Fix-it

Although I knew Toady Tyler at school I only knew him rather vaguely, like everyone else – that is until he decided he wanted something and then he would be all over you. Well, I am afraid he moved in not more than a couple of miles from me, and worse still, he discovered where I live, and my telephone number too.

He is exactly the same as he always was, but this time he usually unleashes his charm offensives on the telephone. "Hello, Torky old boy, I was just wondering if I could borrow your extension ladders. Would you mind bringing them round on your old jalopy? I have just bought a new car and don't want to take any risks – you know what I mean!" And so it goes on.

Only last week he was on the phone again. Apparently his lawnmower was involved in a fatal accident with his favourite garden gnome, and I had to lend him mine so he could cut the grass ready for the barbecue to which he did not bother to invite me. Enough was enough and so I made a resolution to turn my answerphone on permanently so that the next time Toady rings he will get nothing more out of me than the sound of my voice.

However, something happened in the last few days that made me have second thoughts. I put my little boat up for sale at an exorbitant price, knowing full well that buyers are offering peanuts for boats like mine. Quite out of the blue someone made me an offer at little less than I was asking, so I started to storm the gates of heaven to ensure that the deal would go though. Regrettably it did not because the buyer fell ill and had to withdraw.

When I was offered peanuts by a local greengrocer I was able to work him up to a reasonable price that all depended on the surveyor's report. If he did not diagnose a dreaded boat disease known as osmosis then I was home and dry. If he did I was sunk, probably quite literally. Once again I stormed the gates of heaven until the surveyor's report gave my boat a clean bill of health and I could relax.

I was having a drink with a friend to celebrate the sale when I said quite involuntarily, "Thank God for that." Suddenly I realised I had not. It was then that I saw that I was not any better than Toady Tyler who I was always grumbling about. I treated God in exactly the same way as Toady treated me. I was always quick to get a direct line to him when no one else could help me, but the moment I had what I wanted I forgot all about him and regularly forgot to thank him. Even when I did, the time I gave for saying 'thank you' was never more than a fraction of the time I gave for begging him to give me what I rarely really needed, and even more rarely deserved.

If I have always thought Toady Tyler was an out-and-out scrounger, interested only in himself and what he could get out of others, what must God think of me? I have been treating him for years as Toady treated me. I could not blame God if he turned on his answerphone permanently and did not even bother to listen to my prayers which are usually petitions anyway.

Dietrich Bonhoeffer coined the phrase 'the God of the gaps' to describe the sort of person we try to turn God into – the One we turn to to fill in the gaps in our lives that no one else can fill, to satisfy the needs that no one else can satisfy. We treat him like the mechanic who we never think about or care about until the car breaks down, or the plumber we hardly pass the time of day with until we have a burst pipe.

Of course the gospels tell us to ask for our needs, but they tell us something else too. They tell us that God actually wants us to become more than mere beggars, he wants us to become his friends. Now friends are not always seeking to exploit one another. They do not just get in touch with you or give you a ring or call in when they want something from you, but when they want to see you. When you ring them up they do not say, "Hello, what do you want?" Or when you drop in to see them they do not have to think up excuses for not lending you what they think you have come for. Friends love talking together, sharing news, exchanging views, but most of all they just like being together, even when, or perhaps most of all, when there is nothing particular to say, nothing more important to do than just being together. Friends do not give you things you need just because it gives you pleasure but because it gives them as much pleasure as it gives you. It is not an obligation, it is a joy to share with friends, and they will always give you anything unless they are certain it will do you more harm than good.

I have changed my mind again. I have decided to turn my answerphone off except when I am out. If Toady tries to use me again, as he surely will, so be it. It will help to remind me of how I am always using God. It will help to remind me too of the sort of friendship that God is always offering me, if I can stop thinking of him as 'Mr Fix-it' for long enough to realise what this means.

Chapter 6

The best of all possible starts

I decided to move house at the beginning of the year, so I set off for Winchester to haunt the estate agents for the afternoon. I had hardly arrived when a blue van, throbbing with rock music, screeched to a halt in the parking space beside me. I only had a ten pound note so I was forced to ask Elvis for change or risk being clamped. Although he was busy cramming a drum kit into the back of his van, he dropped everything and emptied his pockets to help me. When it was obvious he could not change my note, he insisted on giving me the thirty pence I needed. "What is the world coming to if we can't help one another," he said.

I was mortified. I simply did not know how to react, so I just mumbled an embarrassed 'thank you', bought my 'pay and display' ticket and stuck it on the car. Two minutes later I pulled off a brilliant sidestep to avoid two National Society for the Prevention of Cruelty to Children collectors and jinked across the road and into the estate agents. I visited every agent in the town without once committing myself.

I went to a building site for lunch. The local paper had announced a cheese and wine reception to celebrate the opening of a new showhouse. While discussing the merits and demerits of having the downstairs cloakroom off the utility room rather than the hall, I was downing glasses of vin de plonk and wolfing as many nibbles as I could lay my hands on. Then I dashed off to the supermarket to scramble for the Saturday night bargains before closing time.

I am not normally such a scrooge. I used to have a reputation for being generous, at least to my friends, but the little windfall from Grandad changed all that. It held out the possibility of escaping from the little square box with plastic windows on the housing estate where I live, escaping from the edge of the industrial estate, from the constant drumming by night from the local factory. But even Grandad's little nest egg was limited. It could stretch to the house of my dreams only with a lot of imagination and lots more scrimping and saving.

I suppose the truth of the matter is that although the house was on the small side, it had all I needed, but it did not really fit in with my self-image. On the other hand, most of my friends whose homes do fit in with their self-images on the outside, have to live like paupers on the inside. Self-images can be very expensive. I began to realise that I could not afford one. I would never be able to travel or eat out, I would not even be able to vote as I would like. There is only one party that promises to keep me in the manner to which I would like to become accustomed.

If my television did not break down that morning and if I had not left my glasses in the showhouse in the afternoon, I would not have spent the evening reviewing that pathetic little performance in Winchester. But I did, and thanks to Elvis it made me think. It made me think I needed to review my daily performances a little more regularly. It made me pray too for the help I needed before my ego became totally out of hand and, apart from anything else, landed me in the debtors' prison instead of the country cottage I was dreaming about.

So I made a Lenten resolution to introduce an examination of conscience into my daily routine, to see if I could strip a few inches off my ego by Easter. Perhaps I am not the one to say it, but I think I made some headway! I discovered I could buy wax earplugs so that I could sleep at night, so I would not need to move after all. If I could only keep my ego down to average size there is no reason why I could not stay there for the rest of my life.

I do not want to start preaching to others but I promise you will never regret it if you just spend a few minutes a day reviewing your performance the previous day. It will do wonders for your ego. Your family will not recognise you in a week or two, and you may even find you have some money to spare for those who have far more important things to worry about than their self-image.

It was the first time I ever kept a Lenten resolution all the way through Lent, so I decided to try to keep it for good. I have never managed to keep it up every day, but when I become too remiss I am always reminded of it at Sunday Mass, and so I try again the following week. I know that seeing the man I am will not give me the strength to become the man I ought to be, but at least it makes me turn to the only One who can give me that strength.

St Paul said this is the best possible of all starts, so that is something. After all, you are going nowhere if you do not know where to start!

Chapter 7

With thanks to Jumbo Jackson

I freely chose to go to boarding school and only resented it on Saturday nights. When other teenagers were going out to enjoy themselves we had to suffer two hours of study, shepherd's pie, spotted dick, and half an hour's choir practice for high Mass on the Sunday morning. The only way we could get in on the action was by smuggling in as many bottles as we could afford for a party in the tuck shop after the lights went out.

Jumbo Jackson had the idea to smuggle in the booze from the film he saw at half-term. It was the story of how two British officers escaped from their prison camp by walking out of the main gates dressed as Gestapo guards. The boy who drew the short straw would walk out of the main school gates dressed in blacks, with a homemade dog collar around his neck, and make for the nearest off-licence.

I met Jumbo at an old boys' reunion ten years later. He was propping up the bar with a pint of Pepsi in his hand. When I had finished ragging him and reminding him of the spectacular feats that got him crowned king of the revels he looked a little embarrassed and told me that he was an alcoholic.

I was mortified. I did not know what to say or how to react. Was it my fault? After all, I was always the one who egged him on to drink more than he should. He was quick to reassure me and said it had nothing to do with me. He had been married for four years and had two small children when everything came to a head. He came home blotto as usual, to have yet another row with his wife. He had picked up the baby and was threatening to put her in the washing machine and turn it on when he slipped and caught the child's head on the edge of the draining board. The poor child had to have five stitches in her face.

The next day he went screaming for help to Alcoholics Anonymous. He told me how he had to stand up at their meeting and admit that he was an alcoholic. He told me of the help that he received, and of the twelve steps that every member has to make to help come to terms with the problem. He gave me a pamphlet explaining the twelve steps, and I still have it. The first step is that they have to admit they are powerless to help themselves, that alone their lives have become unmanageable. The second is that they have to come to believe in a power greater than their own, who alone can help them. And the third is that they have to turn their lives over to God as 'they understand him'.

It struck me later that Jumbo's predicament, that of the alcoholic, is a perfect example of the spiritual mess that we are all in if we could only see it. The fact that our plight is not so obviously dramatic is a mixed blessing. Sometimes we need something dramatic to shake us into some sense of reality, so that we can see ourselves for what we are, stripped of all the falsity and pretension with which we so often surround ourselves.

There can be no renewal in our lives unless we are able to see and admit our own utter weakness and our past failures, as the alcoholic has to. Once we begin to see this and experience how helpless we are, then we can start to appreciate the fundamental principle of the spiritual life – namely, that we cannot go a single step forward without God. The Gospel does not say, "Without me you will not be able to get very far". It says, "Without me you have no power to do anything."

The trouble is we do not really believe this except as a purely academic principle of theology that we regularly disregard in our day-to-day lives. We beat our breasts with a sponge, pour out a drink and slump down in front of the television. If we truly believed it, then we would scream out for help, as Jumbo did. We would turn to God as he did and find the time to open ourselves to his healing power through prayer. The space and time that we try to find in our daily lives for prayer is the practical sign of our sincere acceptance of our own weakness and of our total need for God.

It was humility and prayer that were not just the saving of Jumbo's marriage, but the making of it. When I saw the man he had become, and the success that he and his wife had made of their life together, I felt it was time to do something about my own life.

Despite those parties in the tuck shop I have never had a drink problem myself but I have had plenty of others, so I decided to use those twelve steps as a sort of meditation throughout the following Lent. Then I tried to make a sincere and honest confession at the end of it. I knew I had a long way to go, but thanks to Jumbo's example I was able to make a new start that Lent instead of drifting further into the spiritual apathy that was threatening to engulf me.

Chapter 8

Know thyself

Though Mac was a millionaire he never let a week go by without visiting someone in need. I went to his house only once, to pick up a microwave he wanted to give to a family who were going through hard times. He seemed to be a bit embarrassed by the comparative luxury in which he lived, though his house was in no way showy or ostentatious.

There was nothing to give the impression that its owner was particularly religious, though I happened to know there was an 'inner room' beneath the stairs that he used for prayer. There was, however, an icon on one of the walls of the living room with two simple photographs framed in wood on either side of it. One was of a poorly thatched Hebridean black house where he had been brought up with five brothers and four sisters, the other was a Glasgow pub where he was brought down by an addiction that dogged him all his life. He had put them in a place of prominence so that he would never forget where he came from.

We cannot all look back on a childhood of grinding poverty, or even a misspent youth when we ended up in the gutter, as apparently Mac had done, but we can look back in shame at the behaviour that mocks the ideals we hoped to live by. The truth of the matter is we have all made a mess of our lives, as we can see, if we have the courage to look back at the past with the sort of clarity that comes from trying to draw closer to God. That is why saints always seem to see their past as it really was, while sinners rarely do.

I am not suggesting that we should morbidly pick over the past looking for muck to make us miserable, but we should look for the truth so that we can be set free and filled with joy. I do not suppose that all the saints were a barrel of laughs, but nor were they misery-bags either. They were more often than not full of a profound joy that most of us rarely experience. It is the joy that can come from seeing and accepting the truth of our past and the faults and failings that have made us stumble our way into the present, where the past can alone be redeemed.

Many of us have experienced the profound peace and joy that comes after what used to be called 'a good confession'. I remember the joy I experienced years ago after making a general confession during a retreat. But these have long since gone out of fashion. What was called a 'review of life' came into fashion in the seventies; this did much the same thing but in a more systematic way. The importance of these opportunities to look back at the past, in a spiritual rather than a psychological way, is to set us free to turn to God as never before, because we have humbly admitted, as never before, what we have been, what we are and what, or rather Who, we need more than anyone else. That is why a life that may have shamed us and spiritually maimed us in the past can in fact redeem us in the present, if we have the courage to face it for what it was and face ourselves for what it has made of us.

This is what Lent is for. It is a spiritual desert where we take the opportunity to seek out some sort of solitude for at least some of the time, as our spiritual forefathers did. It is here that we try to draw closer to God, who is found only through a profound self-knowledge into which he first leads us. The Desert Fathers insisted time and time again that solitude is not a self-indulgence that separates us from the needs of others, but a means of opening us to them more than ever before. This is what I learned from

Mac who never preached to anyone, other than by the way he lived his life and served others who were not as fortunate as himself.

If we find that some physical deprivation helps us to be more aware of our human weakness and spiritual need then we will see why fasting has always been considered an important part of Lent. Too many people think that it is only meant to show how strong they are so they give up the first time they fail. But its true purpose is to show how weak we are and to encourage the humility that is needed to begin again no matter how many times we fall. The weakness that is experienced in failure and the humility we need to begin again lead to the true self-knowledge and the prayer that cries out for help to the God who never fails to give it.

Chapter 9

Instructions not included

It was on Christmas day that I first met Mac. He was wheeling some severely handicapped people into the carol service. He was, or, as he would say, is an alcoholic who insisted that his affliction was his greatest gift. Without it he would never have faced the man he tried to hide from himself and from others, and the past that could so easily have prevented him from growing into the person who made such a deep and lasting impression on me and on many others.

Twenty years later to the day I met another alcoholic who made a deep impression on me. We did not meet at a carol service but at Christmas dinner. She sat next to me and much to my annoyance won the most glamorous paper hat of all – and from my cracker! Fortunately I had the good grace to admire her when she embellished it further and placed it on her head because, as I discovered later, she was one of the most sought-after international supermodels. You see I am not a regular reader of Vogue or Marie Claire, or any of the other fashion magazines for that matter, and the only catwalk that interests me is from our neighbour's back door to my bird table.

But if you are into fashion, the name Paula Hamilton may ring a few bells. If not you will surely remember that sophisticated commercial for Volkswagen in which Paula portrays a haughty aristocratic femme fatale who is prepared to throw away her jewelry and furs and everything else, save the key to her beloved and indispensable VW. When I beat her at Trivial Pursuits I never thought I would hear from her again but as promised, she sent me a copy of her book Instructions

Not Included. It is a most moving account of a young woman whose unhappy childhood helped augment her desire for fame and fortune.

Her lack of self-esteem made her believe that her success was primarily due to her guile and subterfuge rather than her gifted personality coupled with the perfect size, shape and form that is mandatory for any model. But something further is required to become a supermodel and achieve fame; it is that subtle, hardly definable something that eludes description. It has something to do with a unique but natural blend of inner and outer beauty that shines through the quality of the eyes and plays around the mouth even when it is at rest.

It is a quality that attracts not only the welcome attention of the camera but the unwelcome attention of those who want to use and abuse the person for their own ends. Paula's desire to please the camera, and the unwelcome attentions of those who only wanted to exploit her, led to great suffering from both anorexia and bulimia, from terrible feelings of rejection and worthlessness, and from the effects of the soft and hard drugs that seemed to fill the inner emptiness, at least for a while. It was only after a superhuman effort to overcome cocaine that she gradually realised that the real addiction even her greatest efforts could not overcome was alcohol. It was this addiction that finally attracted the sort of media attention that could have ended her career.

There is no mention in her book of any religious influences in her early or later years, nor will you find any religious language let alone the sort of jargon that so often characterizes the 'born-again Christian'. There is nevertheless a profound spiritual message that is never preached.

It is the message that is at the heart of the Easter mystery, revealing that God's power can find full scope in human weakness to transform and transfigure it. All that is required is that we recognise our weakness and turn our lives over to God to enable him to do in us what he has already done in the human weakness that Jesus freely chose to accept. This has been done and can be done again and again in anyone who is forced to face the depth of their human inadequacy.

Just as St Paul discovered that his greatest gift was his weakness, so Paula realised the same, thanking God for the addiction that finally made her reach out for the help she needed. It was then that she received the power, not just to face her past, but to look forward to the future that has now become possible because the one to whom she has opened her life can do great things for her and through her for others.

Chapter 10

Mac and the art of motor car maintenance

I once had a car for more than six months before I even looked at its engine. Motor car maintenance is not one of my strong points. If I have any trouble with the car or see it coming I usually start thinking about getting another one. So when the only motor mechanic I have ever trusted told me my beloved Ford Escort would expire within days if it did not have an engine transplant I rushed to trade it in before the inevitable. After four days of talking to the local dealers my poor brain was ready for a transplant too.

It reminded me of the day I decided to take the spiritual life seriously. I did not have a clue what to do so I read every book I could lay my hands on and sat at the feet of one guru after another. But I only became more and more mixed up. They all seemed to be saying different things. One emphasised the importance of observing the ten commandments and the new one that summed up all the others. Another stressed the theological and moral virtues and the corporal works of mercy. Yet another put the emphasis on the gifts of the Holy Spirit and how we should attain them. And so it went on.

At the time I could not have named all the ten commandments, at least not in the right order, and I did not have a clue what the theological and moral virtues were, never mind the gifts of the Holy Spirit. I almost gave up in despair. It was far more complicated than buying a new car. I felt I needed a spiritual theologian to explain everything to me, to show me where I should be going and to recommend a guru who would help me get there. If I had not met

Mac I would never have moved forward, but his lifelong problem gave him the insight that he shared with me, and this gave clarity and order to what was so complicated before.

After years of fighting a losing battle against alcoholism, and losing his wife, his family and most of his friends, he discovered the great secret that enabled him to rise from the gutter where he had eventually ended up. With the help of Alcoholics Anonymous he came to realise that he could not help himself until he accepted his own weakness and his need for some sort of transcendent power that could give him the strength to do what was impossible without it. His religious upbringing enabled him to see that the transcendent power was the personal God he was taught to believe in by the monks at Ampleforth where he went to school. The gospel that he had not read for years described in detail how this power could enter into human weakness and transform it. It was the story of how Jesus accepted this human weakness in order to show us how weakness can be turned to our advantage by exposing it to the power of God who alone can transform it.

The power of God is the Holy Spirit. When weak human beings begin to open themselves to the action of the Holy Spirit and begin to experience it as it enters into them, as Jesus did throughout his life, then they can start to live a spiritual life as he did. When the spirit of God begins to suffuse our human spirit and strengthen it then everything seems possible that appeared impossible before. Now it becomes possible to observe the commandments that were so difficult to observe before, to live a virtuous life as Jesus did and to experience the gifts of the Holy Spirit for oneself and for others, even if unable to name any of them. That is what Jesus meant when he said, "First seek

God and his Kingdom and then everything else will be given to you."

As soon as he saw this Mac made a tiny 'inner room' for himself under the stairs in his own home, to which he could retire to pray as Jesus did throughout his life. It was here more than anywhere else that he experienced the divine Spirit entering into and permeating his own, with the help and strength he needed.

Without this strength he could never have given up the habit of a lifetime, let alone begin to learn new habits that would enable him to follow the man he had come to admire more than any other. He told me to begin by reading the Gospel of St Luke, often called the Gospel of the Holy Spirit, so that I could see for myself how Jesus was transformed by the same power that could transform me. His clear and simple insight enabled me to see with clarity what I never saw before.

As a person opens themselves to experience the same spirit that entered into Jesus, then like him their weak human spirit will be suffused and then activated with the divine, making all things possible that were quite impossible before.

Chapter 11

A man in a million

The most impressive retreat I ever attended was given by the Orthodox Archbishop, Anthony Bloom. He began by telling the story of a retired headmistress who offered her services to him as his chauffeur.

As they were returning home one Monday afternoon she stopped the car in Kensington to pick up her new glasses from the optician and proceeded to try them out for the remainder of the journey. It was less than a mile but it turned out to be the most terrifying journey either of them ever made. The poor chauffeur got out of the car shaking all over, opened her handbag, took out her driving licence and ceremoniously ripped it into little pieces.

"I will never drive again." she said. "Why ever not?" asked the Archbishop. "Because," she replied, "there is so much traffic on the road!"

He suggested that we should begin the retreat by praying for better sight, that is, better spiritual sight to see the moral morass within us. The more clearly we are able to see what separates us from God then the sooner we will come to know our need of the help that only he can give us.

The most accurate translation of the first beatitude to be found in the New English Version of the Bible is not "Blessed are the poor in spirit", but rather, "Blessed are those who know their need of God". This is always God's first gift to those who seriously want to deepen their spiritual life. It is a gift that makes us aware of our complete dependence on the God who is utterly beyond the reach of the arrogant and the proud.

St Luke's Gospel is often called, 'The Gospel of the Poor', because the writer shows so clearly that Jesus came first for the poor and needy and preached primarily to them. The expression 'poor' in the gospel does not refer to how much money we have in our wallet or in our bank account, but to how much humility we have in our hearts and how deeply therefore we 'know our need of God'. The depth at which this need is experienced will always be measured by the quality of the prayer that rises from it to the only One who can help us.

That is why St Luke's Gospel is also called 'The Gospel of Prayer'. Luke stresses the importance of prayer for those who know their 'need of God' more clearly than the other gospel writers. It is also known as 'The Gospel of the Holy Spirit' because of the emphasis placed on the action of the Holy Spirit. It explains how the Spirit works most perfectly in those whose eyes are open to see their need of God and whose hearts and minds are open to receive him. 'The Gospel of Mary' is perhaps the commonest and most popular title of all those given to this gospel. Luke shows that Mary is the most perfect example of those who are 'poor' and so 'know their need of God'. She is open and receptive at all times to the workings of his Holy Spirit. The combination of her humble prayer, her fiat and the action of the Holy Spirit means that she becomes a Mother to Christ and then completes her motherhood by selflessly giving him to the world that he came to serve.

These four titles contain within them a theology of St Luke's Gospel in miniature and a simple summary of the spiritual life. Those who have the courage to pray, "Lord that we may see," and then have the humility to accept what they see, can become mothers to Christ as their prayer enables the Holy Spirit to do for them in some measure what has already been done in full measure in Mary.

In the Acts of the Apostles, sometimes called St Luke's 'Second Gospel', we see what happened when Jesus was born again by the power of the Holy Spirit in those 'poor' whom he chose to take his message to the world. Their message bore fruit because they carried in their own persons something of the person whose words they preached.

I think that is why that particular retreat made such a deep impression on me. It was not so much what Anthony Bloom said, it was what he was. It was a case of 'the singer and the song'. I always tend to judge a person by whether or not they allow me to be myself. I am always wary when I feel the need to put on an act to make myself acceptable to others. You only need to put on an act in front of another performer.

Anthony Bloom was not a performer. That is why I could be myself and feel accepted for what I was, and then be inspired to become the sort of person he was. He was one of the best examples I have ever met of the 'poor in spirit', a humble man, a man of prayer, who has enabled the Holy Spirit to embody within him a clearly discernible semblance of the Man whose message he preaches.

Chapter 12

The call to pregnancy

The man in front of me had only one arm and no legs. It was the same man who sat in front of me the Christmas before, and the Christmas before that. Almost all the congregation were severely handicapped apart from the Dominican sisters who came to sing carols. The Mass was to be said by a Franciscan priest who came each year to Grange Farm to celebrate Christmas with the patients who were looked after at their holiday home by 'The Winged Fellowship'.

It was evident that the priest was lost for words when it was time for the sermon. Perhaps he had prepared one that seemed somehow inappropriate when he was faced by a congregation who were all severely handicapped or sick. So he asked for help.

After only a short pause the man in front of me asked him to say a few words about giving. He said he knew that Christmas was supposed to be a celebration of giving because of what God has given us, but, he said, we who are handicapped feel embarrassed because we have so little to give.

The priest was obviously deeply moved but he was yet again lost for words until an elderly woman in a wheelchair suddenly said, "But surely Christmas is more about receiving then giving?" The priest paused and thought about it for a few moments before a glimmer of recognition began to spread over his face. "You're right," he said. "That is why Mary is so important because she shows us how to receive. She shows that it is only the lowly, the humble, those who know their need of God who can receive the One she received and gave birth to. Without her humility there would have been no good news because the good news is not primarily a body of truths but a body full of love."

Later when that body full of love began to preach, he said quite openly that he wanted everyone to be his mother, to bear and give birth to him as Mary did. Only by imitating her humility could this birth be brought about by the same Holy Spirit who conceived the Christ Child within her. That is why Jesus directed all his preaching to the poor, the lowly, those who knew their need of what only he could give, because only they could receive in some measure what Mary received in fuller measure.

Mary could receive in fuller measure because there was no sin in her, no arrogance, no pride that could prevent God's love finding full scope within her. That is the point of the theme of repentance that sounds like the recurring beat of a drum throughout the liturgy of advent. It is to remind us that unless we turn away from the pride and prejudice that keeps the Holy Spirit out of our lives, he can never enter into them as he entered into Mary's life.

No matter where or when we begin the spiritual journey, we will never get very far unless some way, somehow, we come to the point of knowing, not just with our minds but with every fibre of our being, our utter and total need for God. It is a painful journey because it always involves spiritual, psychological, or physical suffering or a combination of all three.

Nobody likes to be made humble for whatever reason or in whatever way, but be sure about this, it is the only way for those of us who are not immaculately conceived, to be conceived by the same Holy Spirit who conceived Jesus in Mary. Being humbled and made to feel helpless does not automatically open a person to God. As often as not it can open a person to self-pity, to depression and even despair. But with good will and God's grace it can lead a person to turn, to receive in ever fuller measure something of the fullness of grace that enabled Christ to be conceived in Mary. Every Christian, male or female, is called to be made pregnant by the power of the Holy Spirit so that they can become mothers to Christ in order that his life can grow ever more fully within them and then, like Mary, they can give him to the world.

It was a good ad lib sermon thanks to the promptings of one of the most severely handicapped people I have ever met. She thanked the priest for confirming what she had evidently discovered for herself through personal experience. I thanked her too for helping me realise for the first time that Christmas is more about receiving than giving, or rather about first receiving before we have anything, or Anyone, to give to others.

Chapter 13

Famous for fifteen minutes

We could not help being amused when we heard that the Bishop could not go to Lourdes because he sprained his ankle. But the Headmaster was not amused when he heard that he had decided to grace our speech day instead. It was customary to put on some sort of entertainment when the Bishop was presiding over the proceedings, but nothing had been prepared, so it was decided at the last minute to produce a Shakespearean anthology.

It would comprise two comic scenes sandwiched between three serious ones. There were no budding actors in my class so we all drew lots to play the part of Henry V and the lot fell on me. Day after day I practised extravagant gestures in front of a full-length mirror. At the dress rehearsal I got far more laughs than the gravedigger from Hamlet and the porter from Macbeth put together. I put it down to the dramatic tension that I was able to generate. Had they never seen great Shakespearean acting before?

The English master said nothing until a matter of moments before I stepped on stage on the big day. Then he took me by the arm and said, "Now listen here, Torkington. Forget about that pathetic little performance last night. If you act like that today, Reverend Mother will take you back to the convent school and make you head girl! You're supposed to be a warrior king not a fairy queen! This isn't a stage, it's a battlefield. They are not fifth formers, they are your men who are tired and exhausted. They have been storming the town all day and achieved nothing. They have seen their friends falling at their side, heard the cries of the wounded and they are all but defeated. Get out there, rouse 'em, rally them for one more attack before it's too late!"

And with those words he pushed me on to the stage with one hand and pulled the curtains back with the other. To this day I do not know what happened, I just remember saying, "Once more into the breech, dear friends, once more," but I cannot remember what happened next until that thunderous applause at the end that I will never forget.

Even my worst enemies thought it was a marvellous performance. Monsignor thought I was drunk, and the Bishop wanted to sign me up for the diocese. "Put him in the pulpit," he said, "and he'll make Savonarola sound like a Simple Simon." But they had it all wrong. It was not a performance at all. I was not acting - it was for real. Somehow the English master managed to inspire me with the spirit of the man who trounced the

French at Agincourt. I was famous for fifteen minutes, not because I was a good actor, but because for fifteen minutes I became a living reincarnation of the greatest warrior king in English history.

I have always seen that 'performance' as a key moment in my life because it gave me the most important spiritual insight that I ever had. It enabled me to see that you can only really become like someone else, and act and behave as they do, by being inspired by the same spirit that inspired them. If you try to copy them as I tried to copy Henry in the first place then you will certainly end up caricaturing them, and people will laugh and call you a ham. If you try to copy Jesus Christ in that way they will more likely call you a hypocrite.

There is only one way to imitate him and that is not by copying his outward behaviour, but by copying the way in which he opened himself to be inspired by the Spirit who conceived him in the first place. If we can only open ourselves to receive the same Spirit that conceived him, then we can be inspired from within to become perfect as he was perfect.

Nobody will ever succeed in becoming a Christlike person by studying his perfect human behaviour and then by trying to replicate it in their own. It just cannot be done, failure is inevitable, and if you think you have succeeded then others will have other thoughts: at best they will think you are a second-rate actor, at worst a first-rate hypocrite.

The only way to become a Christlike person is to allow the same Spirit who animated and inspired him to animate and inspire us also. Prayer is the word used by Christian tradition to describe how serious-minded believers open themselves to this Spirit. As the selfsame Spirit who made Jesus into a perfect human being begins to make us into perfect human beings, then perfect human behaviour follows naturally as a matter of course without a hint of hypocrisy.

If you have found this insight as helpful as I have over the years, do not thank me, thank the Bishop's twisted ankle and the desperation of a young English master who inspired me for fifteen minutes to do what I have never been able to do since.

Chapter 14

The sixty-four-thousand-dollar question

Moral leadership courses were all the rage when I was a student, so I went to the local retreat centre with high expectations. The priest who was leading the course taught us how to picture gospel scenes, using our imagination wherever possible to focus our attention on the exemplary behaviour of Jesus. Then the members of the groups he set up would discuss the virtues they discovered and list them in order of priority. By the end of the course we had produced a sort of league table of all the most important virtues.

"Now," said the priest, "If you want to become an exemplary Christian you must try to acquire for yourselves the virtues that we have discovered embodied in the life of our Blessed Lord." As a sort of afterthought he enquired if anyone would like to ask him any questions. He did not really expect any; in those days people did not question much and after all the formula had been well tried and the outcome was predictable, even if the participants thought otherwise. So the priest looked slightly apprehensive when one of the students stood up, but only slightly. After all, this would most likely be a vote of thanks. But it was not.

"Well, Father," said the young man, "I would like to thank you and the other priest for all you've done to make this course a success. However, I can only speak for myself when I say that I have found it very disappointing. You see, in general I can see more or less how I ought to behave if I want to become an exemplary Christian, but that is not my main problem. My main problem is that I am unable to do it. I find myself in the same dilemma as

St Paul. He could see how he ought to behave, and he had to admit that he did not have the inner power and strength to do it.

"Surely this is the sixty-four-thousand-dollar question that we all want answering. Where do we go to receive the inner power and strength to make us into the sort of people we would like to be? It is a question that this course does not seriously attempt to answer, at least that is how it appears to me."

"May I suggest that you come to our follow-up course, 'Tools of the Trade' when we show how to acquire the self-same virtues that we have been discerning in the life of our Blessed Lord. And secondly, may I emphasise the importance of the grace of God, without which we will never be able to generate authentic Christian virtue."

The young man stood up again. "I followed the course 'Tools of the Trade' last year," he said. "That is why I am concerned with the whole approach used in these moral leadership courses. It only pays lip service to the action of God's grace in the spiritual life, while placing all the practical emphasis on human methods and techniques. I am not a scripture scholar nor a theologian, but I do have a doctorate in philosophy – Greek philosophy, to be more precise. That enables me to see that these courses have as much if not more in common with Greek moralism than with a Christian mysticism that is surely at the heart of the gospel.

"Forgive me for being so blunt, Father, but these courses do not reflect the spirit of the gospels at all, but rather the spirit of the Renaissance when Greek moral philosophy was introduced into Christian spirituality, giving it an emphasis that is completely absent from the scriptures. Please can we have the gospels in the future, not a pagan moralism thinly disguised as Christianity?"

The young philosopher sat next to me on the coach journey back to college and I had a fascinating conversation with him. He explained to me that Jesus was not primarily a moral philosopher who had come to detail the way in which we are to love God and our neighbour, but a mystic who came to give us the power to do it. He does this by showing us in the example of his own life how to expose ourselves to the inner power and strength that will alone enable us to love God perfectly and our neighbour as God loves us.

I never looked at the gospel in that way before. My companion's clear and incisive reasoning led me into my first real conversion experience. It was a conversion to the religion that I was brought up and educated in, but which I never fully understood before. The clear waters of the gospels had been muddied by a moralism that owed more to Socrates of Athens than to Jesus of Nazareth.

Chapter 15

The art of the impossible

I have often been accused of being too airy-fairy, of overemphasizing the mystical at the expense of the moral, of stressing so much the importance of Christian prayer that I all too often neglect the importance of Christian action. But the truth of the matter is we might be brimming over with ideas and ideals for ourselves and for humanity, but something further is required if we are going to be more than armchair idealists.

It is all very well to talk about caring for the deprived and the neglected, stamping out colour prejudice, helping the third world, creating authentic community, but it is all pie-in-the-sky unless our hearts are changed radically from within by God's love. This is the only power that can change us, and prayer is the only direct means we have of coming into contact with that power.

The point I am trying to make is that by and large all of us know what we ought to do in our day-to-day relationships with others, our problem is that we do not do it. The main problem is not with our heads but with our hearts. It does not take a spiritual Einstein to name and analyse the perfect qualities that should characterise the ideal otherconsidering person, but that will not get us very far. It is all very well to say that we ought to listen to others with genuine concern, to enter into their lives, to try to feel for and with them, but how on earth do we do this? That is the question. Books have been written in an attempt to analyse the model moral behaviour of Jesus, to put all his actions under a microscope so that we can examine in detail his exemplary dealings with others, but how will this help us to do the same? They may fill us with admiration and inspire us to follow—that is their strong point—but their weak point is they never show us how!

It is the same with the lives of the saints. It is assumed as a matter of course that the mere portrayal of heroic virtue is enough. It is based on the misguided belief that if you can present perfect human behaviour in an attractive enough way, it will somehow enable us to generate the necessary inner strength to follow suit and acquire the same moral qualities for ourselves.

The plain fact is that it is impossible to do so—at least not by human endeavour alone, and not with any lasting effect. Christianity is not primarily concerned with presenting or analysing every detail of perfect human behaviour. It is primarily concerned with communicating the love that will alone enable us to be perfectly human. Once love has made us perfectly human then perfect human behaviour follows as a matter of course. The gospels show us how this happened in Christ's life and promise that it will happen in ours too, if we only allow God's love to possess us as it possessed him.

Our main concern is to be permeated by the love that was the mainspring of his every action, to be penetrated by the Spirit that was the source of all he said and did. If you want to play the part of Henry V, it is not enough to learn his lines and rehearse the gestures that you think would be appropriate to fit them. You may get away with this sort of thing in the annual school play but it would be laughed out of court in a serious production. The role would appear for what it was—disjointed, inarticulate and contrived. Henry V would appear more as a caricature than a genuine character. If you want to play the part effectively you must not only learn the words, but you must also study the man, get to know him, enter into his mind through empathy, if not love, and let his spirit enter into yours. Then you will be able to play the part convincingly because he will come alive again in you, as you are animated by his spirit. When this takes place you will no longer need to work out artificial gestures because the movements will happen naturally, as if they were your own, because they will be your own.

The gospels invite us not just to copy a Man who completely embodies perfect human behaviour but urges us repeatedly to enter into that Man and to allow him to enter into us, so that he can animate us with his spirit. Then the perfect human behaviour that we see embodied in him will gradually be embodied in us, in everything we say and everything we do. But without him and the love he came to communicate we will have no power to do anything. There is nothing airy-fairy about this because it is the very essence of the gospel of the Lord.

Chapter 16

The man with no arms or legs

Those of you who have retired, or who may be thinking of retiring or dreaming of retiring, may be interested to know of a place with no taxation at all, or at least no taxation as we know it. No income tax, no value added tax and no capital gains tax! But before you up sticks and stake your claim to a retirement home in this exclusive tax haven, I am sorry to have to inform you that it no longer exists!

I am talking about ancient Athens, whose citizens were free of the financial furies that pursue us throughout our lives, and even after our deaths, to exact payment for whatever we earn or spend or even give away to others. It all sounds too good to be true, because we know that even utopians need roads and bridges, civic buildings, and public amenities. They need to protect themselves too with defences, with armies and navies, and those things do not pay for themselves.

So how did they do it? They invented a unique method of public service that required every citizen to be responsible for financing one major public project once in their lifetime. It may be erecting a statue to one of the gods, building a temple or equipping a battle trireme to defend their shores. When they had financed the project they would be considered free of any other financial responsibility to their fellow citizens. This act of public service performed by one person for the whole community was called their 'liturgy'.

When the first Greek converts were told what Jesus Christ did, and was continuing to do, not just for his own people but for all peoples, they said that was the greatest 'liturgy' that anyone had ever performed. It was the greatest act of public service performed by one person for the good of all humankind. However, these converts did not just want to be bystanders merely admiring what he did for others, they wanted to become participators by choosing to share in his unique act of selflessness. So when they asked what they had to do to participate in Jesus' timeless act of public service they were first told, and then taught, how to welcome into their lives the same Spirit that filled and animated him to enable them to do for others what he did, and still does. Whether they were converts or not, the first thing that was taught to any believer was not how to love God or how to love their neighbour, but how to receive the love of God that would enable them to love him in return and to love their neighbour also.

This was something that had to be taught again and again through what came to be called the 'liturgical year'. Each year, through words, signs and symbols, every important stage in the life of Christ, from his birth to his ascension was celebrated by the believers. In this way they could see and experience for themselves how Jesus received the same love that they needed to receive. Then through the sacraments and deep personal prayer they would both receive and be sustained by this love that would take them up ever more completely, not just into his life, but into his action, not in the past, but in the present. As each liturgical year was celebrated, the believer could enter more and more deeply into the liturgy of Christ, the great public service that he performed and is continually performing in the world that he came to serve.

During the Second World War a parish church was almost completely obliterated at the end of an intense bombing raid by enemy planes. Only the wall behind the main altar remained intact with the crucifix still hanging on it, although the arms and legs of Christ had been blown off his body. When the church was rebuilt two years after the end of hostilities the parish priest refused to restore the crucifix which was still in its original position behind the altar. At the dedication of the restored church he told his parishioners that the cross would remain without arms or legs as a permanent reminder of how they must now become the arms and legs of Christ to take his message and hand it on to the world he chose to serve through them.

Perhaps the story can be a permanent reminder for us today, not just of the great liturgy of love that reached its high point on the cross many years ago, but of our liturgy of love as we try to participate in his selfless sacrifice and endeavour to take to and share with others what we have received. There is no greater public service we can perform than this.

Chapter 17

Dead men tell no lies

Every year we used to have a film on Founder's Day, paid for by the Headmaster but chosen by us. That particular year the distributor deeply regretted that our chosen film, 'Jack the Ripper', was unavailable and sent 'Last Holiday' instead.

It was set in pre-war Britain and told the story of a young commercial traveller who specialised in selling agricultural machinery in the south of England. At the beginning of the film the young man, played by Alec Guinness, was told by his doctor that he had contracted a rare disease of the spleen and had only six weeks to live. After the initial shock he decided to make the best of it, so he gathered together every penny he had and went for a last holiday in a five-star hotel somewhere on the south coast. Having arrived and changed for dinner he found he could not leave his room. He was completely overawed by the grandeur of the establishment and by the great and the good who patronised it.

Then he suddenly realised that as he was as good as dead to that class-conscious world that had so intimidated him before, he was free from the power it held over him. He did not have to put on an act any longer to make himself acceptable to anyone. He could just be himself, do exactly what he wanted and say just what he thought, whether it was acceptable or whether it was not.

When he bumped into the Minister for Agriculture at the bar he told him just what he thought of the policies that were ruining the farming community. The minister was so impressed by his candour that he offered the man a prestigious job in the ministry, which he declined. Later the young man detailed the faults of the latest combine harvester to its manufacturer whom he met at dinner. The manufacturer immediately offered him a consultancy on the board, which he turned down. And so the film continued, in a similar vein, to its rather bizarre conclusion.

Fr Williams, the projectionist, used the film as subject matter for his sermon the following Sunday. He told us that our baptism meant that we had already died to the same world that had so intimidated the young man in the film, if we only realised it. The confirmation that many of us were about to receive was the ideal time to reflect on what had already happened, so that we could come to terms with that death as the young man did. Then if we were prepared to accept this spiritual death it would lead us into a freedom that we had never known before, in which we would be free to become our true selves, free to stand up for and bear witness to the truth.

Dead men tell no lies he told us, nor can they be bribed by power, position or financial gain. But he warned that people who have the courage to speak the truth are rarely praised or rewarded. He reminded us of what happened to Christ himself and to the martyrs who followed him as they tried to bear witness to the truth as he did.

The combined effect of that film and that sermon made a deep impression on all the boys, several of whom, to my knowledge, suffered in their later life for having the courage of their convictions. One of the boys who later became a Member of Parliament finally lost his seat because he refused to toe the party line on abortion. Another old boy was thrown out of South Africa for preaching against apartheid, when the other members of his religious order pursued a policy of appeasement. A close friend of mine resigned from the police force because his superiors refused to acknowledge his criticisms of unethical methods of interrogation.

I never did see 'Jack the Ripper' but I am sure my life has been none the worse for it. It would have been the worse, however, for not seeing 'Last Holiday' and for not hearing what Fr Williams made of it. It has helped me over the years to come to terms with the meaning of my baptism even if I have never fully died, as I should, to the world that still bribes and corrupts me.

Let us hope I can make a better job of dying in the future to the world that corrupted me, along with so many others, in the past. I have tried to speak out here and there as others have done, but I know no one will ever hear me till I am so dead and buried with Christ that I can live fully by the same life that raised him from the dead. It is only then that I will have the inner strength to flout the world that has so often floored me. Perhaps then I can make a stand for the standards that Christ lived and died for, instead of living by the standards of the world that knows the price of everything and the value of nothing.

Chapter 18

Henry the confessor

My granny would not think of receiving communion without first going to confession the day before, even though I have never known her do anything worse than put too much salt in the porridge.

In my lifetime the practice has changed from times when you would need the patience of Job to get into the confessional at Christmas or Easter, to the occasion when one priest I could name actually fell asleep in the box during Holy Week for lack of custom. I should know because I was there when he suddenly woke up and pretended he had been listening all the time to what I knew he had not. If he had he would have given me more than three Hail Mary's!

A good friend of mine, Henry, who proudly proclaims himself a dyed-in-the-wool traditionalist, said he is horrified at how the customary practice of confession has been reduced to a mockery of what it used to be. The trouble is that Henry knows very little about tradition. He like many just know a lot about the tradition they assimilated between 'mewling and puking in their nurse's arms' and the time when they finally stopped 'creeping like snails unwillingly to school'.

Sometimes it was a tradition that developed only in the generation or two that preceded them, if that. Look at how confessional practice has changed, for instance, since my granny was putting too much salt in the porridge. We may think she was too strict but many of her forebears would have considered her too lax. I dumb-founded my friend by authoritatively informing him that the first confessional box was erected in 1517. I do not know why that date suddenly sprang up from the other ecclesiastical trivia that clutters my mind, but it did. However he was not impressed; in fact he did not believe me. Neither did he believe me when I said that large numbers of early Christians did not go to confession at all.

I told him that St Ambrose used to advise the young to put off confession as long as they could because once they had been they could not go again. Once and once alone was all that was permitted in the Early Church. When Henry still would not believe me I gave him a few books to read to put him right. I made sure that one was written by a Cardinal and another by a Monsignor whose orthodoxy was beyond all question.

When I met him a few weeks later I met a new man who had been chastened by history. He said he never realised that private confession as we know it today was all but unknown for the first eight centuries of

Christianity. Of course there were penitents and there was confession but it was only for three or four mega-sized sins and was usually made in public in front of the whole congregation. Now if I was a confessor and had to deal with people like Henry in 'the box' I would not make them recite Hail Mary's. I would make them read liberal doses of history for their sins and we would all be the better off for it. Church history gives a true perspective that can broaden the mind and soften the hearts of the most dogmatic ecclesiastical bores. It can make them quite huggable at the kiss of peace, if you go in for that sort of thing.

Henry is not quite huggable yet, but you have no idea how much he has changed since being converted to history. When I met him a few weeks ago he said he was no longer a traditionalist but a traditionist. "Tradition," he said, "is the living voice of the dead. Traditionalism is the dead voice of the living." However, he admitted quite frankly that he does not want to bring back public confession even if it was commonplace in the Early Church, nor has he made any major changes to his own confessional practices. He is still as regular as ever, but he said he sees everything from a different perspective now.

He sees more clearly than ever before how sin not only separates him from God but from others too, not just from his own family but from the wider family that arrogant narrow-mindedness made him scorn before. History has also taught him humility that has enabled him to see and admit his sins for what they are instead of hiding behind the well-worn cliché that he hid behind for years. If he does not go to confession before he goes to Mass he would not think of missing out on communion, but he arrives early enough to prepare himself for what he took for granted before.

Outwardly you would not notice much change in Henry's practice, but he has changed a lot within, thanks to the One who can speak through history to those who are humble enough to hear.

Chapter 19

It's only a wave of a wand away

I suppose psychologists would call them a dysfunctional family, and I suppose they would be right. I have known them for years and visited them from time to time over the Christmas period. I will not mention their name because some of you may know them and I do not want to betray confidences. It is the father's second marriage and it is turning out to be something of a disaster.

I do not really like taking sides, but it is evident to me that the real troublemakers are the stepdaughters. They are two of the most self-centred women I have ever met, and they make their stepfather's life a misery. But there is someone else who suffers even more: it is his own daughter by his first wife. If it was not for her I think the two sisters would tear each other apart, but instead they turn all their spitefullness and jealousy on her.

The father is not free of blame. I have always thought he should stand up for her more, but he never does. I think he is just weak, though he claims he does not want to be seen as favouring his own flesh and blood. But the truth of the matter is, far from being favoured in any way she is reduced to being little more than an unpaid servant in her own home, who rarely leaves the kitchen where she is at everyone's' beck and call.

Every Christmas that I have revisited this family I have been horrified at how the poor girl has been treated, but all is forgotten the moment her fairy godmother waves her magic wand and changes poor Cinderella's fortunes for good. Although I have always enjoyed it when the pumpkin is changed into a beautiful carriage, and the mice into fine white horses to carry her to the ball, I always wonder why they were necessary in the first place. You see, they have no sooner left than there is another wave of the wand and the drab and dreary kitchen is itself changed into the magnificent ballroom, resplendent with dazzling lights and colourful furnishings. The wonderful world she dreamt about in that gloomy workplace was in fact there all the time, no further than her fairy godmother's love away.

That spectacular transformation scene has always symbolised for me that other world which we all desire to enter if all our hopes and dreams could be realised. It is not a million miles away. It is where we are now, no matter how ordinary and commonplace our surroundings may seem. If we can be as open as Cinderella was to the kind of love that she received we can enter into that world without moving an inch from where we are. The fairy godmother's transforming love has always been a reminder to me of that other, even greater love that can change the world we live in now to the world we are destined to live in to eternity, if only for a while. That is why I have always enjoyed Cinderella more than any other pantomime at Christmas.

When it is all over and I come away filled with delight at the fun and the magic of it all, it never leaves me flat. It leaves me thinking that it is not just make-believe, not if you really believe in the power of love. It makes me realise that no matter where I am or what I am doing there is another more exciting world into which I can be transported without going anywhere or without even stopping what I am doing.

This other world surrounds us at all times like another dimension that is invisible to those whose hearts and minds have been closed by greed and self-seeking. Once we have learnt the secret of how to open ourselves to perfect love, then a far more profound transformation can take place than the one that happens on stage which is only an illusion anyway. It can transform us and the world around us by entering into us so that we can begin to see everything differently, as it really is, in the light of the love that we have opened ourselves to receive.

I suppose every story has a moral, as the Mock Turtle said to Alice – or was it the Cheshire Cat, or the White Rabbit? Anyway the moral of Cinderella's story for me has always been that love can change everything and everyone, even the casualty of a dysfunctional family. Now if that is not a good enough moral with which to end the Christmas season, I do not know what is. I know it may sound like a jaded old cliché to those who are bored to death by talk of the only thing that can bring them back to life, but that is their problem. Let us hope and pray that it will never be ours.

Chapter 20

Where time touched eternity

I am not a wimp when it comes to weather. You cannot afford to be if you want to go birdwatching in the Western Isles. But when two holidays on the run are literally washed away without leaving the merest mark upon the memory, you begin to wonder what the birdlife is like on the Costa del Sol!

That is what I was beginning to think about as I sat in the little cottage on the island of Barra surrounded by some of the most beautiful scenery that can be seen, if I could trust the word of my Hebridean hosts. It was their word against that of a thick, all-enveloping mist that had spent every minute of my holiday with me. I do not usually get angry with the weather, but I did that night, the last night I thought I would ever stay in that God-forsaken place.

I banked up the peat fire, chucked all the local guidebooks into the bin, scribbled a note to my host cancelling my booking for the following year, and settled down with a book for the evening. When I woke up at five o'clock next morning, the whole room was filled with an uncanny red glow that created a sense of expectancy as if some strange, unearthly event was about to take place.

The scene I saw as I stared out of my window will haunt me for the rest of my life. A long jagged inlet came to a point not more than fifty yards from my cottage. It looked like a twisted dagger of brand new metal, polished to perfection and shining with the savage beauty of newly spilt blood. My eyes followed the shape of the blade back to its source in the sea, a sea that spread out to the horizon like a vast frozen lake, glazed with deep crimson death. The smooth, motionless water mirrored its own bloody complexion upon the surrounding countryside. The sky was hidden behind thick, evenly spreads clouds that acted as a perfect backcloth, receiving the same eerie light which suffused the entire scene with varying degrees of intensity.

It was as if I was transported back in time to some prehistoric landscape long before the primeval forests began to sprawl over the earth before the birth of the most elemental forms of life. I dressed and sat by the water's edge utterly entranced by what I saw. As the sun rose, it gradually disappeared behind the clouds. The morning's magic had cast its spell and disappeared, leaving behind a heavily overcast day with a touch of freshness in the wind that threatened rain.

I do not know how long I lingered there by the side of the sea, lost in the memory of what I saw, absorbed by a sweet melancholic sadness that is worth all the joys of a manmade world ten times over. I was eventually distracted by a large female rabbit watching over two of her offspring. They were skipping and scampering along the foreshore in front of me. Suddenly the mother stiffened. She became tense and nervous, and before I knew what was happening all three had disappeared into their burrow. My own sense of awareness was heightened too, as if the subtle sense of presence that had touched me so gently before became embodied in some new, vital, but indefinable manifestation that momentarily gripped me with fear and awe.

Instinctively I turned to my right and gazed upwards into the sky. To my amazement and delight I saw a huge golden eagle no more than a hundred yards away and as many feet from the ground. Its head was set hard towards the prevailing wind that blew in over the headland. Its vast wings were spread out imperiously to leave no doubt that here in person was the Lord of the Isles. He remained almost motionless, staring impassively out to sea.

There was a hush. A sense of quiet enveloped the whole island. The blades of grass seemed to waver against their will, and even the little cottage appeared to lower itself upon its haunches, not daring to move or flex the merest muscle that might attract the attention of the mighty bird of prey.

Then all eyes stared incredulously. Even the breeze held its breath as a tattered old crow, the island idiot, fluttered and flapped its way upwards and above the great bird. In a grotesque attempt at a dive, the clumsy creature had the audacity to try to mob the eagle single-handed. Just one stroke of those terrible talons would have been enough to send the simpleton senseless to the ground, but the great Lord of the Isles was not going to demean himself. The slightest movement of his great wings was enough to send the imbecile sprawling downwards in humiliating disarray.

Twice more the pathetic creature attempted to repeat his dangerous ploy with the same embarrassing result each time; but enough was enough. Without warning the mighty eagle began to rise higher and higher over the headland, with hardly perceptible motion, until he was more than a thousand feet up, far beyond the idiot's reach. Then, before I could get back to the cottage for my binoculars, he had disappeared over Eriskay, heading towards the rugged coastline of Uist.

I remained in a sort of mystical daze for the rest of that day, so that to this day I hardly remember the journey home. But I did not forget to pack the guidebooks I threw away the evening before, or to destroy the letter I left for my host; nor did I forget the cairn I built by the side of the sea, where time had touched eternity and made a mystic of a very ordinary man like me.

Chapter 21

Pride and prejudice

As usual the media ended the year with a deluge of flashbacks and nominations: personality of the year, film of the year, book of the year, quote of the year – the list seemed endless. It made me look back too and wonder which of my offerings to the Catholic Herald would be voted article of the year if MORI had nothing better to do.

I know I would be looking for a few slaps on the back to boost my ego and recharge my enthusiasm for the year ahead, but it would be a genuine help too, to know what readers find most helpful. Anyway, I decided to do a poll of my own, so I asked some friends of mine to tell me what they thought and to ask around to find what others thought, and then I reread a few of the letters I had received – solely in the interests of scientific research, you understand!

One particular article was mentioned more than any other. It was the story of that disastrous holiday in the Outer Hebrides that you have just read, when it rained every day and made me so miserable that I made a solemn vow never to return to that land of mist and monotonous rain. Many readers were able to identify with that experience because they had similar ones themselves – experiences that had stained their memories and remained with them throughout their lives as brief and fleeting moments when they 'felt' the touch of God.

Many years after that event I was giving a talk to over a hundred Kenyans and Ugandans from a dozen or more different tribes at a place called Nkokonjeru, a few miles north of Lake Victoria. I talked at length of the experience that I had all those years before and of its effect on my life. When I finished speaking an uncharacteristic silence enveloped the whole assembly and stopped me in my tracks. The almost eerie silence made me feel I had misjudged my audience. How could they possibly understand what I was talking about? How could they understand that experience which had deeply influenced me on a remote Hebridean island many years before and thousands of miles away from their world?

My confidence suddenly left me and I floundered. "I'm so sorry," I stammered. "I feel you're not with me. Do you know what I'm trying to say?" I will never forget their response. They knew exactly what I was trying to say, exactly what I was talking about. I had completely misunderstood their silence which spoke of their profound sensitivity to the sacred that they had all experienced many more times than the man who was speaking to them; the patronising man from the so-called civilised world whose sense of the sacred had been gradually suffocated by pseudo-sophistication. As one they nodded, probably slightly irritated that I should question their understanding, that I should delay in explaining further what they knew far more about than me.

I once had the arrogance to think that my experience on the Island of Barra, and similar experiences that I had elsewhere on the moors, in the mountains and through the music that meant so much to me, was unique. I now know that they were not unique to me, but universal, felt by everyone whose sense of wonder has not been blunted by the brash materialist world that has lost its sense of value.

These spiritual insights are not ends in themselves but means that will lead all who respond to them into an ever-fuller experience of the One whose beauty is so ancient and yet so new. Any authentic spiritual journey begins with God's sacred touch that reaches out to us through the world that was shaped by his hand, and through the melodies of man's own making that reflect its beauty. We must not look to the poets for our guidance on this journey, but to the mystics. The inspiration of the poets enables them to say so well what we have already experienced, but the mystics show us the way forward to receive the fullest possible embrace of the One who has already touched us, though briefly, with 'the finger of his right hand'.

If we would open our ears to them and to their world we must first learn to close our ears to our own world and to the street cries of those who would seduce us. Only then can we give our fullest possible attention to the 'one thing necessary', and the one Person necessary who embodies all the beauty, all the goodness and all the truth of the world that was shaped by his hand from the beginning.

Chapter 22

The Agony and the Ecstasy

The first homework I was set in the lower fourth was to write an eight verse poem on any theme I cared to choose. I was horrified: poetry was for girls or sissies, not for me. I had just put on my first pair of long trousers and I had no intention of celebrating the arrival of my manhood with a poem!

It was only later when we were introduced to the metaphysical poets and the romantics that I had second thoughts. At first glance I had put Wordsworth in the 'for girls only' category, until the English master described the mysticism that smouldered beneath the surface of his works. It struck a chord with me and made me want to read more of his poetry and that of the romantics who followed him.

My family owned a cottage in a remote spot high up in the Yorkshire Dales where we used to spend most of our summer holidays. I would spend hours and hours alone, roaming wherever I wanted, looking for my favourite birds of prey – the kestrels, sparrowhawks, merlins, and harriers. The fells bordered on to the Lake District so I knew the world that Wordsworth wrote about. I also knew something of the experience of what he called the 'numinous' that pervaded all, and whose presence became almost tangible in precious moments that remain in the memory for the rest of your life.

The natural mysticism that excited me in the English class meant far more to me than the religious class where we had to learn large chunks of the catechism off by heart. It meant far more to me than the Mass and the sacraments, for that matter. I could not see how everything fitted together – that is, until I read St Augustine.

I was bored during the annual school retreat and thought I would add a little spice to my spiritual education by reading the confessions of someone I heard had been a bit of a lady's man in his youth! It was then I found what I had not expected – that everything did fit together after all.

St Augustine discovered the same sort of experience that I had, and that Wordsworth and other romantics who followed him had too, but he went further. The 'Someone' whose presence could be experienced through creation was the Creator – that much I guessed for myself. But St Augustine went on to say that if God's presence could be experienced through the works of creation how much more perfectly could his presence be experienced through the Masterwork of creation – the presence of God made flesh and blood in Jesus Christ. This was the point of a new departure for St Augustine, as it was for the mystics who preceded him and those who would follow him.

What is but a brief and fleeting experience that the poets try to capture in verse eventually becomes a more permanent experience for the mystics whose lives are gradually transformed by what, or rather by Who they have experienced. St Augustine knew that you cannot love someone unless you know them, so he began to study the sacred texts of the scriptures, ruminating on and relishing every word he read, as the Desert Fathers did before him. The spaces between people are bridged by words for those who know how to listen. True prayer takes on a new meaning when it becomes more concerned with listening than with speaking, listening to the words of the Masterwork of creation. When he speaks, his words penetrate the inner being, not just with meaning but with love.

Gradually as St Augustine began to experience this love reaching out to envelop his whole being he began to respond in the language of love, as he cried from the depths of his being:

"Late have I loved you, Oh Beauty so ancient and so new; late have I loved You!"

When everything had been said that he needed to or could say, he found all he wanted to do was to be still, to savour in silence what he had received, to gaze upon the One who had ravished him, in a profound contemplative stillness. As D. H. Lawrence put it, "Speech travels between the separate parts, but in the perfect one there is a perfect silence of bliss." What St Augustine glimpsed many years before with the poets and the natural mystics, finally reached its consummation here on earth in, with, and through the Masterwork of God's creation, Jesus Christ – the All in all.

When the ecstasy came it did not come without the agony, it came through the agony. A heart that is restless until it rests in God has first to undergo a baptism of fire; it has to be purified and refined through suffering. Only the pure of heart can 'see' God, and so the man who began his spiritual journey praying, "Lord, make me pure but not yet!" would have to spend years of purgatory on earth before he could experience more permanently something of the heaven on earth for which he yearned. Anyone who would follow St Augustine must be in no doubt about the agony as well as the ecstasy that purifies a restless heart that would rest in God.

Perhaps the poets are 'sissies' after all if they never rise from their poetry to journey on like Augustine, to experience in full what they have been trying to capture in part in poetry that is as transitory as the experiences that inspired it.

Chapter 23

A perpendicular paradise

Received wisdom had taught me that virtue was its own reward and one should seek no other, until my local supermarket persuaded me otherwise. A simple system of points per purchase enabled them to reward the virtue of loyalty with a galaxy of glittering prizes. A hundred points could earn you a whole packet of sour cream and onion crisps, five hundred a 'Mr Nosey' book, while eight hundred could be exchanged for a whole 'Mr Blobby' celebration cake to share with your friends.

With difficulty I managed to restrain myself until the end of Lent when, would you believe it, I had amassed enough points to have a two-for-the-price-of-one holiday break in Dorset at a hotel with a sauna, a

Turkish bath, and an indoor pool. Although the short break was primarily designed to placate my body that had grumbled its way through the rigors of the penitential season, its better half was 'surprised by joy' when, by accident rather than design, I wandered into Sherborne Abbey immediately after the full English breakfast promised by the brochure.

Even my body paused momentarily from relishing what it had received to enjoy something of what raised my soul above itself. I had heard of Sherborne Abbey before and had been told it was worth visiting. I also knew that St Stephen Harding had been brought up there before moving to Molesme from where he founded the Cistercian Order at Citeaux, but nothing had prepared me for the overall effect of this architectural gem.

St Stephen would never have seen the glory of what Sherborne Abbey finally became because it was only after a fire destroyed its interior in the early part of the fifteenth century that it was restored in the Perpendicular style. It was the first complete church to be decorated in the new English style, one that I first saw at King's College Cambridge when I was a schoolboy. I had just finished reading D. H. Lawrence's description of the glories of Lincoln Cathedral in The Rainbow and this made me look at church architecture with new eyes. Through those eyes my soul began to soar with the magnificent vaulting and find an architectural and spiritual satisfaction that made me vow to visit all the great gothic cathedrals of England. It is a vow that I have still not fulfilled but have recently renewed thanks to Sherborne Abbey.

A friend whose daughter had lapsed from her faith despite an excellent convent school education had found her faith restored when, as an undergraduate at Cambridge, she attended evensong in King's College

Chapel. The combination of the solemnity with which the service was conducted, the unique sound of that incomparable choir, and the sheer transcendent beauty of the chapel helped raise her soul with the magnificent perpendicular vaulting to rest in some incommunicable way with the One for whom that masterpiece had been built in the first place.

The great gothic cathedrals were intended to raise hearts and minds to the transcendental majesty of God and at the same time make worshippers aware of their smallness, weakness, and unworthiness so that they could be led to discover the true prayer of humility, that he who is mighty can do great things in them. But the new Perpendicular style, that was England's greatest gift to European architecture, induced a further response that is essential to any authentic Christian spirituality. Added to the awe-inspiring transcendence of God that was embodied in these great medieval masterpieces was a sense of wonder at the beauty of God expressed in the delicate soaring splendour of the Perpendicular style. Now the humble of heart could be moved not only by awe at the transcendent majesty of God but by love at his unsurpassed beauty and enabled to experience something of the height and depth and length and breadth of love that surpasses all understanding.

I hope you do not think I have been trying to promote the material and spiritual benefits of loyalty to your local supermarket because, quite frankly, there are none. For the person who, unlike me, is prepared to shop around, disloyalty pays far greater financial dividends. But I would like to thank my local Supermarket for unwittingly providing the means for a holiday I may never otherwise have taken, and for a profound spiritual experience that made me renew the vow I made all those years before.

Chapter 24

In an English country garden

Miss Holt's idea of heaven was a thousand miles away from mine. On special days she used to produce a giant-sized book full of glossy pictures that told the story of the Old Testament, but sadly she rarely went further than Adam and Eve in their garden paradise. Those who were good were promised an ever more beautiful garden to play in when God would take them to enjoy his heavenly paradise in the next life.

The trouble was, I hated gardens! Everyone said we had a lovely garden at home, but I did not. No cricket, no football and no rugby were allowed for fear of wearing out the lawn or decapitating the plants or smashing the panes in the greenhouse. Heaven for me would be more like sailing in that fantastic boat with Noah and all the animals, or seeing fire and brimstone consume Sodom and Gomorrah, while Lot's wife was turned to salt, or watching Pharoah and his armies being swallowed up in the Red Sea; but Miss Holt never seemed to get that far.

Instead of telling us what heaven was like the student teacher asked us to tell him, so I did. I told him that heaven for me would be like spending endless hours at my favourite funfair with pockets full of money so that I could go on the ghost train whenever I wanted, and the big wheel, and the whip, and the caterpillar, and then ride on the big dipper till I had the courage to sit in the front carriage. He said I was right, and if that made me feel really happy then that is how I would feel when I went to heaven, and he did not even add the words, 'if I was a good boy'.

When I discovered girls in my teens I soon discovered a new idea of what heaven could be like, but being a good boy seemed to be more complicated than before. Then I had a new idea of heaven when I began climbing mountains in the Cairngorms, and then another when I started sailing in the Solent, and many more as my life unfolded, but being a good boy seemed to get more and more difficult the older I became. It became so difficult that I thought I would have to settle for having my heaven on earth just in case I did not have it later. After all, a bird in the hand and all that!

Anyway, what I want to tell you and Miss Holt, if she is still around, is that her idea of heaven was right after all. My salad days are over now, and so are my days of mountaineering and sailing too, and all the other enthusiasms that once gave me a glimpse of the heaven hereafter through my brief experiences of heaven on earth. You see, there is nothing I like more than gardening now - not my own, you understand; that is far too strenuous, but other people's. I am far more interested in being than doing these days!

Not all that long ago I followed the sign for Mottisfont just a few miles north of Romsey in Hampshire. Before the Reformation it was an Augustinian priory but now it houses the National Collection of Old Roses. As you enter the garden you are asked to refrain from smoking because the roses are renowned for their scent, which is augmented by the delicious perfume of different varieties of lavender and honeysuckle. When I visited it earlier in the year I was slightly disappointed, but when I went back at the end of June, when almost all the roses were out, it was to enter my idea of paradise on earth.

Although the sun shone brightly in a clear blue sky there was a gentle breeze which raised the different scents until they merged and mingled and distributed their heavenly aroma throughout this miniature paradise. It reminded me of what is called in Hebrew the Ruach, the gentle breeze that blew in the cool of the evening in the first paradise and was identified with the breath of God. It was this Holy Breath that breathed life into all things that were made, and into the man, with whom God walked and talked in the Ruach of the evening.

Although there were hundreds of people at Mottisfont, there was an aura of silence, a sense of awe. Everyone seemed to realise that they were privileged to share in some mysterious but tangible way in something of the first paradise for which we were all created, and to glimpse in some small way the paradise for which we are all destined. Funfairs are now my idea of hell on earth! Miss Holt was right after all. Special gardens like Mottisfont, are more like heaven on earth than anything else I know. Let us hope that at last I will become a 'good boy' so that I can finally arrive at the place for which we have all been made from the beginning, and in which we can walk and talk with God in the cool of the evening in his endless sabbath rest.

Chapter 25

The two in one

Shortly after I left school for good I was taken to see Aida at the Royal Opera House, Covent Garden. The music was not entirely new to me but the overall effect of the production was beyond all my expectations. When the curtain fell at the end of the grand march I was literally entranced. I did not want to go to the crush bar with the others for a discussion on the merits or demerits of the current production. I just wanted to be transported back into the solitude of my own room to savour what I had received.

Somehow, through the medium of the composer's music I was able to experience something of the beauty, something of the glory and the majesty of God, and I did not want the experience to be dissipated by meaningless claptrap. Beautiful scenery, moving pieces of music or artistic masterpieces had similar effects on me in the past. Later on, my spiritual director called these experiences 'mystical premonitions', because that is what they are. They are experiences in advance of the mystical awareness of God through his creation or the human creations that mirror God's works. These premonitions eventually become more commonplace for the true contemplative who has been sensitised to God's presence through a long purification.

The reason why those of us who have not been purified do not experience his loving presence all the time is because we are so lost in ourselves. Then all of a sudden we are taken out of ourselves by the combination of some powerful external stimulus and an inner receptivity of mind and heart that enables us to experience for a short time the love of God that is there all the time. These experiences actuate a sort of holy restlessness that enables a person to understand what St Augustine meant when he said, "Our hearts are restless until they rest in you." They prompt people to search for the One who has touched them, to experience in ever fuller measure the love without measure that has briefly reached out to them.

At the time I mistakenly understood these experiences as a call to religious life or to the priesthood. But they are not a call to a particular way of life, rather to the fullness of life that is for all. Long before my father met my mother he knew all about these experiences. His geography master had interested him in astronomy and he used to stay up all hours on the school roof gazing at the stars. To begin with his interest was purely academic; to end with it was purely mystical. He did not bother with the telescope when the grandeur and majesty of the heavens spoke to him and touched him with the sort of knowledge that you cannot find in books. He did not, however, interpret this experience and others that were similar to mine as a call to religious life, nor did it ever cross his mind for a moment that he should become a priest. But he did want to know more fully and experience more deeply the One whose presence had touched him in those mysterious moments that made him mourn for his maker.

That presence reached out to him in a new and unexpected way the day he met my mother. She was to be for him an even greater and more perfect embodiment of the One he was searching for. It is not man but mankind that is created in the image and likeness of God, man, and woman together, who in their mutual loving manifest the most perfect embodiment of God's loving. The masculine and the feminine that are perfectly balanced as one in God, are manifested as two on earth, so that man and woman, in entering into the other through love, experience God in a unique embodiment.

In coming to know and love my mother, my father came to experience through her something of the beauty, the goodness and the truth of God clothed in a feminine form that excited his heart, his mind and his body and led him on into an experience in which God's presence made itself felt more fully than ever before. It was an experience that became more and more perfect as, with the passing years, the selfishness that still kept them apart was gradually purified through the suffering and self-sacrifice involved in bringing up a family together.

The love that was generated and then deepened by their testing purifications enabled them to receive and minister to each other an ever more profound love that would overflow on to their own family and on to other families too who were inspired by their lifelong love for each other. Though they are both dead now their loving goes on for there is no end to the journey into the infinite sea of love into which we all desire to plunge ourselves.

The reward of the traveller is to go on travelling, the solace of the searcher is to go on searching, for there is no end to this journey this side of eternity.

Chapter 26

No need to be alarmed

The alarm clock that had served me faithfully for over twenty years expired without warning two hours before it should have woken me for one of the most important appointments of my life. It was the summer of 1982 and I was due to take up my position in Heaton Park, Manchester to commentate on Pope John Paul II's papal Mass for the BBC.

The producer was beside himself when I arrived almost twenty minutes late. When I explained the reason for my delay he looked at me incredulously. "I can't believe it," he said, as if to himself. "You're a Catholic and I'm a pagan, and yet you're late because you put your faith in an alarm clock, and I'm on time because I put my faith in the Holy Souls."

He explained how his wife, a devout Catholic, always woke him dead on time and without fail thanks to the Holy Souls in whose power of intercession she had an unerring belief. I too had practised a similar devotion before the Second Vatican Council had made me feel I should temper many of the pious beliefs with which I had grown up and led me to play down the traditional teaching on purgatory in the interests of ecumenical dialogue. I used to spend hours on the feast of All Souls trudging from one church to another to pray for the poor unfortunates who could not pray for themselves.

There used to be a famous museum in Rome that exhibited the various horrors that Holy Souls would have to endure before they could enter into heavenly bliss. All the tortures so common in medieval Europe were represented in order to encourage pilgrims to the eternal city to part with their money in exchange for indulgences that would ease their passage through purgatory, or even bypass it totally, while contributing to the architectural splendour of the city they had come to visit. It is not surprising that people protested when the financial success of the 'chamber of horrors' in Rome inspired the unscrupulous to extend the practice of seeking financial gain for spiritual favours to the rest of the Roman Church. If right-minded people had not protested, and if there were no Protestants, I hate to think what would have happened. Perhaps there would have been no Catholic Counter-Reformation, or it might have come too late.

Perhaps we owe a debt of gratitude to the Protestants, who can hardly be blamed for viewing the Catholic teaching on purgatory with continued skepticism. Personally I never had any problems with believing in purgatory. Even though my emotional attachment to a childhood devotion waned in the aftermath of Vatican II, my mental conviction has never varied. I can at least understand those people whose belief in a loving God makes them question whether or not there can be a hell, but not whether or not there can be a purgatory.

All who have experienced being loved know how it makes them feel unworthy of what they receive and aware as never before of the personal faults and failings that stand in love's way. Lovers who journey on together, come what may, are gradually purified by the love that they generate until nothing prevents the fullest possible union that they desire on earth. But the fullest possible union that we all desire in heaven can be brought about only by the most perfect love of all, a love that reaches out to us through human love and gradually purifies those who receive it. Those whose purification is complete this side of the grave will not have to wait the other side of the grave for the union that is the deepest desire of all. Those whose purification is not complete are traditionally called Holy Souls and the place or state where they receive the love that completes them is called purgatory.

Anyone who has experienced love knows how it is redemptive and how it lays bare the unbearable to purify it away. That is why redemptive love always involves much suffering no matter where it has to be endured, as any married couple know from experience. When freely accepted it not only mirrors the redemptive suffering of Christ but unites the believer to him in the most perfect prayer he ever made. That is why the prayers of the Holy Souls have always been considered so powerful throughout Christian tradition. It is their continued acceptance of what we so regularly shrink from that makes their prayer for us more potent than other prayers.

I declined the alarm clock that my producer offered me. If a pagan did not need one, nor did I. I thought it was about time that I returned to the faith in those who, unexpectedly, inspired him. I have turned to them often since then and they have done far more for me than merely wake me up in the morning—though I have never been late since!

Chapter 27

The cradle of contemplation

I know that the greatest gift I have ever been given is the love of God that first came to me through the close and intimate loving of my mother. It gave me the inner strength and security I needed to begin my life knowing that I was loved and therefore lovable, even if I have not always made full use of the start my mother gave me.

Interestingly enough one of the first books I ever read on mystical prayer was by St Bonaventure, who said that contemplation is first learnt at the mother's breast. A beautiful picture of the Madonna and Child had been placed alongside his words, ensuring that they would be enshrined not just in my mind but in my imagination for the rest of my life. Jesus had already been fed; he had a surfeit of human food and was just leaning lovingly against his mother's breast. His eyes gazed contentedly into the distance, laden with the love that enveloped him. Everyone who has been blessed with a mother's tender loving-kindness has experienced contemplation, even if they cannot remember it. It is an experience that will return later in life, at first in brief glimpses and then in a more permanent and abiding way for the believer who perseveres in prayer beyond first beginnings.

Although you may have first experienced contemplation at your mother's breast, as you begin to grow you become 'busy about many things' as natural curiosity keeps your mind occupied for many years to come. Even the prayer learned at your mother's knee tends to be busy too—busy asking for so many things that seem to be beyond the human grasp. But the time comes when the divine touch that you first experienced through the touch of your mother moves you again at a time when you least expect it. It may be amidst all the fun and gaiety of a party with your friends. Suddenly the finger of God reaches out and touches you. Amid the hubbub a stillness descends so that you feel you do not belong where you are. You experience a pull to be alone and to be still. You yearn for something or Someone higher, nobler, and more fulfilling. It is the call to contemplation.

It may happen when you are standing on the seashore watching as the sun sets and ignites the sky and the sea with colors that will stain your memory for a lifetime. Suddenly there is a sense of presence that the poets try to capture in verse. It envelops your whole being and remains even when you close your eyes. When the sun has finally set you walk home entranced as if in a dream. God is beauty, harmony, truth, and goodness. When you come into contact with any of these you can encounter the touch of God. It may be in the countryside, at the sea or in the mountains. It may happen in a picture gallery, a concert hall, or an opera house. Whenever it occurs it opens up a deep yearning in your heart for the One who has touched you and you come to understand for yourself what St Augustine meant when he said that our hearts will be restless until they rest in God.

A prayer life that before consisted mainly of asking for things, of petitions, now seems to be insignificant as the heart yearns to experience more fully, more deeply and more completely the Someone who has searched you out and who calls you onward into the unknown. St Augustine had this sort of experience before he even became a Christian and it prompted him to set out on a spiritual quest that led him to Christ, as he describes in one of the most memorable passages of his Confessions.

"When first I knew you, you lifted me up so that I might see that there was something to see, but that I was not yet the man to see it. And you beat back the weakness of my gaze, blazing upon me too strongly, and I was shaken with love and with dread. You called and cried to me and broke open my deafness and you sent forth your beams and shone upon me and chased away my blindness. You breathed fragrance upon me, and I drew in my breath, and do now pant for you. I tasted you, and now hunger and thirst for you. You touched me, and I have burned for your peace. So I set about finding a way to gain the strength that was necessary for enjoying you. And I could not find it until I embraced the mediator between God and man, the man Jesus Christ."

Augustine came to see and understand that if the beauty, the harmony, the truth, and the goodness of God can reach out and touch us through his works in creation, how much more can they reach out and touch us through the Masterwork of God's creation, Jesus Christ. He is the fullest possible flesh and blood embodiment of God's goodness, beauty, and truth. It was to Jesus Christ that all Augustine's searching finally led him, as it will always lead us too.

This is the beginning of the mystic way. It is the point of departure for a person who so far has been little more than a spiritual juvenile. To this point in the spiritual journey they have fed off the faith of their parents and used the prayers they have been taught. Now they experience the touch of God for themselves and feel the call to go forward into the unknown, to savour for themselves the height and the depth, the length and the breadth of God's love that surpasses all understanding*.

*This theme is developed in more detail in David Torkington's book, Wisdom from the Western Isles.

Chapter 28

Three-legged love

I first fell in love when I was eight. Her name was Marion and I thought she was beautiful. She would always become my first catch when we played tag in the playground. Then we would hold hands and chase the others. It was terrific. I usually developed a limp to prolong the most exciting moment of my life—holding hands with Marion. I thought nothing could be more wonderful until we became partners for the three-legged race on sports day. Then I was able to put my arm around her waist and feel her arm around mine.

The next day Fr Wilkin came into our class and said that love was communicated by touch. I was holding hands with Marion under the desk so I went scarlet and everyone looked at us and giggled. I thought he knew all about our love for each other but he had come to talk about someone else's love. He said Jesus handed on the love that God had given him by touch, and taught others to do the same. That is why the Apostles laid hands on people to make them bishops and priests so they could 'hand on' the love of Jesus to everyone else when they baptised and confirmed them.

He also told us that human love can change people. It can make them stronger and nicer to know, so we should imagine how much more the love of Jesus can do. I became very excited. I thought if I could feel Marion's love when she touched me, would it not be marvellous to feel Jesus' love when the Bishop touched me. But I was so disappointed. I felt nothing, I wasn't changed, I did not feel stronger and it did not make me nicer to know either! I felt cheated and I said as much to Fr Hanlon in catechism class six years later. He was very honest. He said he did not feel anything either and he did not know anyone else who felt anything for that matter. But one thing he said he did know for sure, and that was that Jesus' love was given to us whether we felt it or not and one day we would feel it because he knew people who did.

He said that the saints felt it, sometimes so powerfully that it lifted them off the ground and gave them ecstasies and all sorts of things. It made them nice to know too, so nice to know that everybody wanted to know them. What made them sensitive to the love that we cannot feel to begin with, was pure unadulterated selflessness. The more selfless we become the more we will feel the love we have already received like a seed, as it grows and expands to possess every part of us. But selflessness has to be learned slowly and painfully and that is the lesson we have to learn from the saints.

There are two main schools where this lesson can be learned. One is religious life, the other is married life. A medieval mystic and saint called Angela of Foligno described prayer as the Schola Divini Amoris, a school of divine love, because it is the place where the selflessness that opens a person to love can be learned. It is learned like everything else by practice, both inside and outside the prayer-life that enables a person to come to know and love the One whose touch they received many years earlier. As selfishness withers, love grows until it is experienced and savoured in prolonged periods of mystical contemplation. Eventually it seeps out of the times set aside for prayer and overflows into the whole of a person's life, touching all with whom they come into contact.

Although religious life can create an environment in which loving can be learned, it is not a sacrament, whereas married life is. This means that the married couple administer the sacrament to each other in their human loving, transmitting the divine love through touch as surely as did the priests and bishops who baptised and confirmed them in the first place. This does not happen only on their wedding day but on every day when they reach out to each other with selfless, other-considering love. The more selfless their loving becomes, the more they receive and the more perfectly they become open to receive the divine through the human. What they receive from each other will automatically overflow on to their children and on to others with whom they come into contact every day of their lives.

The mystic Angelo of Foligno was a married woman before she continued her spiritual journey in religious life after her husband's death, so she is worth listening to when she warns of the dark nights that are as common in married life as in religious life. If selfless love is finally learned it will not be in spite of dark nights but because of them. Love is purified in those dark moments when one is asked to go on giving without counting the cost, when nothing seems to be given in return. But the cost is not worth counting anyway because it is the price of everything we ever wanted.

The sparks that once flew between Marion and me never did flicker into a common flame. We both went our separate ways. She did not marry or enter the religious life; she did not go to either of the schools I mentioned except the school of suffering, but she has touched more people in her life than anyone else I know.

Chapter 29

The sacrament of touch

I was hauled out of double biology and told that the Rector, Monsignor Duggan, wanted to see me in his private apartment. Both he and Abbot Williams who asked to see me, were dressed in full pontificals as they were about to depart for the bishop's consecration. After the usual boring questions about how I was getting on at school I was allowed to go and returned to biology class just in time to miss out on the reproduction of rabbits. It was the closest the school ever came to explaining the mysteries of life.

When I returned home that night it was to see Abbot Williams again, this time in a totally different environment, attired in vestments more appropriate to the 'domestic church' and the liturgy of the kitchen sink.

He was in his shirt sleeves with an apron around his waist and a dish cloth in his hands. He had chosen to absent himself from the ecclesiastical bun fight at the Grand Hotel in favour of sausage and mash with the Torkington kids who were always pleased to see him, not least because of the chocolate he invariably brought with him.

It was many years later that I learned how much he helped my parents when they first encountered marital problems at around the time of the birth of their first child. He made it clear that he had no expertise as a marriage counsellor and could only offer help of a purely spiritual nature. However, his education on the continent had brought him into contact with theological ideas that were not so commonplace in the more conservative seminaries in Britain. This enabled him to give my parents a positive and rich understanding of their vocation that was sadly denied to the majority of other married couples at the time. He explained to them how love was communicated by touch and how touch was used by the first Apostles to communicate the love they received from Jesus through the laying on of hands. This was one of the means used to transmit that self-same love from generation to generation all the way down to my parents.

When they themselves became sacramental ministers, their touch not only communicated the love they had received to one another, but it became the means by which their love would grow ever deeper and bear fruit. He further explained to them how the emotional limbo that they seemed to have fallen into was not the end of their love but the beginning of a new phase of their life together where true selfless loving could be learned if they would only persevere.

Anyone can give when giving is full of feeling and when it always receives in return, but true love grows gradually only if a person is prepared to go on giving when they feel nothing and seem to receive nothing in return. It is this selfless loving that enables the giver to enter into the selfless love of Jesus and into the sacrifice that finally enabled him to receive in the fullest possible measure, 'love without measure'.

Thanks to Abbot Williams my parents were inspired and encouraged to go on at a time in their marriage when they were tempted to give up. What they finally found, as promised, was that their mutual selfless giving enabled them to receive a strength from each other that totally transcended both of them. Precisely because they had suffered and sacrificed together they became surer and securer in each other's love so that a new and more perfect experience of love gradually began to emerge. There were moments when they were bonded together more profoundly than ever before, when they were united in mind, heart and body in an experience that bordered on the ecstatic. It was an experience that is completely unknown to the person whose idea of love never rises above the purely physical. What was received in those sacred moments led them both into a sort of subtle interior peace, not only immediately after these 'sacred celebrations', but throughout the rest of the day.

When I heard all the wisdom that my parents had learned from Abbot Williams I could not help feeling how much we would all have gained if we could only have had someone like him at the school that prepared us so well for every facet of life, save married life. The reproduction of rabbits is not really the best preparation to become ministers of the sacrament to which most of us were called, but sadly it was almost the only preparation we were given.

Chapter 30

The frog prince

Even viewers who are not particular fans of the English comedian, Harry Enfield, seem to have been amused by his portrayal of a monosyllabic teenage monster. Of course it was a caricature, but all good caricatures contain more than a grain or two of truth, otherwise they wouldn't amuse. People were amused because they could identify with the parents, or with the monster himself because he provided a crude cameo of what they themselves were like in their self-centred teenage days. Harry admitted on the BBC radio program, Desert Island Discs that he was not much better than the monster he portrayed when he terrorised his own parents with antisocial behaviour in the not-so-distant past.

If each weekly episode about our teenage hero was a parody, then the final episode provided the biggest caricature of all and yet once again we could all identify with the dramatic change that took place. Suddenly the frog prince met his princess and was instantly transformed by a love he never knew before. His parents were speechless with disbelief when they saw how the monster who had shattered their domestic bliss suddenly became the normal well-mannered and well-balanced young man they had given up hoping for.

I am not a great believer in instant change, at least not when it is applied to the moral behaviour of a flawed human being, but the sort of change that love can bring about is more effective than any other experience I know. If there is no love to penetrate the cocoon of self-interest that surrounds us, how would anyone ever emerge to become anything like the person God wants us to be?

Perhaps we would never emerge at all, but just degenerate into a society of psychopaths that would destroy itself. It does not matter where love comes from or how a people receive it. If it is genuine love then it comes from God and can lead us towards God, whether we realise it or not. That is what St John meant when he said, "God is love and wherever there is love there is God."

I do not know whether or not Harry Enfield's character realised where the love ultimately came from that saved him from becoming a psychopath, but it nevertheless came from the One who wanted to transform him into his own image and likeness. Now I am not trying to say that his encounter with love transformed him into a saint any more than first love transforms any of us into saints, but it did free him from the possibility of eternal egotism and opened him to a life of giving and receiving. When this love is sustained by the same spirit of sacrifice that was embodied in the life of Jesus then a new person is in the process of being formed. The operative word is 'sustained', because if that mutual loving is not sustained then it will gradually wither and die, leaving the couple bound merely by loveless habit. If their loving is to deepen and gradually destroy in each the selfishness that keeps them from the fuller union that they both desire, they need to turn to the source from whom love gets its name.

'Prayer' is the traditional word used by Christians to describe the act of turning to the love without measure that is needed to sustain any human love. No one will be able to give themselves to each other for richer, for poorer, in sickness and in health, without being open to another love that transcends all and that can gradually transform them by endlessly recharging the human love that is so volatile and unpredictable even in the best of us. That is why the well-worn slogan 'The family that prays together stays together', will never become threadbare. I know from my own experience that the greatest gift I have ever received was the love that my parents had for one another and that overflowed on to me from my earliest years. I know now that the love I received from them owed both its origin and its sustaining power to Another to whom they both turned and prayed.

Bernard Shaw might well have gone over the top when he said that every man over forty is a scoundrel, but it is certainly true that every teenage egotist will revert to type unless the first love that opens him to the possibility of transformation is continually replenished, sustained, and deepened. Jesus came not only to tell us where this love comes from but to show us how to receive it and to demonstrate how it can ultimately transform and transfigure us as it did him. That is why, where there is love there is hope, even for Harry Enfield's monosyllabic monster.

Chapter 31

There is no substitute for experience

I spent most of the seventies running a conference centre in London. In term time we used to run many courses for school groups each lasting for three days. On the fourth day we would invite the teachers in for an assessment and arrange for a guest speaker to address them. If he was available I would always book a certain lecturer from a local teacher training college who was an excellent speaker with a brilliant academic career behind him. The trouble was he had the unfortunate habit of beginning his lectures by questioning his own competence. Sometimes it would become so embarrassing that you would not have blamed his audience if they walked out before he launched into his subject. Fortunately nobody ever did, and when he finally got going he had everybody on the edge of their seats riveted to his every word. He used to mesmerise me, even though I heard him speak time and time again.

After a few years we became very good friends, and so one evening when we'd had a few drinks I asked him why he found it necessary to run himself down in such an embarrassing way. He admitted that he had what psychologists call an insecurity problem. He told me something about himself, about his home background and his upbringing. He explained that he had the best of parents who he knew, without a shadow of doubt, loved him, but because they didn't want to spoil him they deprived him of the close physical contact that he needed in his early years. They never praised him and never showed how proud they were of him despite his brilliant academic achievements. He told me that the love he knew they had for him was worthless as far as he was concerned because he never felt it, never experienced it for himself.

It is not enough to know that you are loved. You must experience being loved or you will end up with a psychological imbalance, a security problem that will dog you for years, if not for the rest of your life. The more a person experiences being loved from their early years then the more secure they become and the more balanced their human personality.

This is why Jesus Christ was the most secure, the most balanced, the most mature and the most perfect human being ever to have walked on the face of this earth. He not only knew that he was loved by his father and by his mother, but he experienced their love supporting him from his earliest years. The baptism in the Jordan was but an external sign for others to see what had

already happened and what would continue to happen at every moment of his life, as the love of his Father, the Holy Spirit, continued to possess him ever more completely.
This was the love at work within him that enabled him to live for others, die for others, rise from death for others and then pour out on all who would receive it the self-same love that made him what he was and what he is now.

At the end of the seventies my friend was offered a lecturing job abroad and I did not see him again for over fifteen years. We met by accident at a summer school a few years ago. I hardly recognised him. He looked the same in appearance, but inside he was a changed man. His lecture was as excellent as ever but it was delivered with far more conviction and authority than before, and without the self-deprecating preamble that I found so embarrassing in the past.

On the evening before the summer school ended I met his wife he had married ten years before and two of his children. Although it was immediately obvious where his new-found security came from, he made it quite clear that without the prayer life that they both tried to build together he'd have been divorced years ago. He said that he was so psychologically handicapped by his first family that his second family would literally never have been born without the help he received in prayer.

Once again I was privileged to see the power of love at work in a weak human being, transforming that person into a semblance of the perfect human being. I remembered the words of John Donne: "Twas much that man was made like God before, but that God should be made like man, much more." This is precisely what happens when human beings are open to receive the same love that filled Jesus.

Although it was in the context of a loving family and through an intimate and personal relationship with a woman, his mother, that Jesus first experienced God's love, that was not in itself enough. It was precisely because he wanted to maintain and deepen what he received that he repeatedly sought solitude in order to open himself to God in profound prayer.

No matter how perfect the family, no matter how loving the relationship, love must always be sought at source to sustain and deepen what is already there. This is what Jesus taught by the example of his own life and what must be put into practice in our lives. When this is done then the love that progressively penetrated him will permeate us also, so that something of his image and likeness will be mirrored in our lives and in the families to which we belong.

Chapter 32

If at first you don't succeed

When he was Abbot of Ampleforth, Cardinal Hume was invited to Rome to take part in a conference on prayer for Benedictine abbots and abbesses from all over the world. Finding himself the leader of a discussion group, he decided to start the ball rolling by inviting the other members of the group to say as simply as possible what they considered to be the essence of prayer.

One said that it simply consisted in having a conversation with God, another said that it was more about listening than anything else, and another felt it involved being open and available to God at every moment. When everyone had their say and Abbot Hume was about to move on, an abbess from Washington stood up at the back and said,

"One moment, you're not getting off the hook so easily, Abbot Hume. What do you say prayer is all about?"

"Well," he replied, "I agree with almost everything that's been said, but I would like to add a little word with which to preface every description of prayer that I've heard. It's the word, trying."

Prayer is trying to have a conversation with God. Prayer is trying to listen to God. Prayer is trying to be open and available to God at all times. Traditionally Dominican spiritual writers have stressed the importance of the mind and of knowledge in this process, whilst Franciscan writers have stressed the importance of the heart and of loving. The truth of the matter is that it is not a case of either/ or, but of both/and. The Benedictine spiritual writer William of St Thierry put it this way: "You can't possibly love someone unless you know them, but you will never really know them unless you love them." And Jesus would add, "When you really love someone you love them with your whole heart and mind and with your whole being."

So perhaps the best definition of prayer is this, if I may paraphrase the old penny catechism. 'Prayer is the raising of the mind, the heart and the whole being to God'. Or, as Cardinal Hume would no doubt put it, prayer consists in trying to raise the heart, the mind and the whole being to God. Now there is no single method of prayer, just different methods. That is why whenever you start to talk about individual methods of prayer it will inevitably prove unhelpful to far more people than it will help. One person may find the Rosary the best method of raising their heart and mind to God, whilst others prefer a well-tried devotional exercise, or set meditation. Others find it easier to talk to God as they would to a friend, or to use the Jesus prayer, or just a simple word, as the author of the Cloud of Unknowing suggests, to keep the heart's gaze fixed upon God.

One of the most ancient forms of prayer is the slow meditative reading of the scriptures, as practiced by the Desert Fathers. They would relish plundering the depths of the sacred texts and the profound experience of being led on by the One who inspired them into the still and silent contemplation of God.

A good spiritual director will know how to recommend different methods and forms of prayer to a person as they pass through different stages of their spiritual development. What may be a great help to a person at the beginning of their journey may be of no help at all later on. What may be beneficial later on may be of no use at the beginning. Good spiritual directors are few and far between and when you do find them they are usually overworked, so the best advice for most of us is to journey on by trial and error if all else fails.

Try some of the suggestions I have made here or the more detailed suggestions in my book Inner Life -A fellow traveller's guide to prayer. A method of prayer is good for you if it helps you here and now to keep trying to raise your heart and mind to God. The moment it no longer helps you to do that, drop it and seek out another that does. Remember the advice of Dom John Chapman, "Pray as you can, not as you can't."

Methods of prayer are only means to an end and the end is to help you get to know God more fully so that you can love him more deeply and receive his love in return. Only this love can transform you into the perfect image and likeness of the One who was raised from the tomb on the first Easter day. Then he can live on in and through you, so that the world may come to believe.

Chapter 33

Practice makes perfect

If your experience of prayer is anything like mine, then take heart, I have good news for you. St Teresa of Avila said that we will always have distractions in prayer, at least, this side of the grave. It is a great mistake to believe that distractions are a sign that you cannot pray, for what does it mean if you have a hundred and one distractions in, say, half an hour? It means that a hundred and one times you have turned away from your distractions and turned back to God. It means that you have repeatedly said no to self and yes to God. You have performed a hundred and one acts of selfless love, that have enabled you to die to the selfishness that rules the best of us.

Prayer is the place where a person freely chooses to go in order to learn the most important lesson that a human being can ever learn, and that is how to love. It is learned by practising selfless loving through prayer in set periods of time put aside for that purpose. There is no mystery about the learning process. It is based on the old principle, 'practice makes perfect'.

If you want to learn how to cook, learn a foreign language or even learn how to drive a car, it takes time and practice. Prayer is no exception. We will never get anywhere in prayer unless we set aside specific periods of time to learn how to act selflessly. Like all other forms of learning it involves performing series after series of selfless actions until a habit of selflessness is formed. That is the only authentic sign of sanctity.

When I was a small boy I fell in love with the violin and pestered my mother for months to buy me one for Christmas.

However, my mother knew her son far better than he knew himself, so instead she bought him a cheap recorder and said, "When you learn to master that, then I'll buy you a violin."

I never did get my violin because I never learned to master the recorder. To this day I can play no more than half-a-dozen simple nursery rhymes because I never submitted myself to the discipline of set times for practice. Prayer is no exception to the rule. If you do not set aside regular times for prayer and stick to them you will go nowhere.

I am frequently asked to advise people what methods of prayer to adopt. Too many fritter away their lives searching for the spiritual equivalent of the philosopher's stone, the magic formula for prayer that will lead them infallibly to mystical contemplation, or to whatever spiritual 'goodies' they have set their hearts on. The truth of the matter is that there is no perfect means of prayer. There are just different means to help different individuals as they keep gently trying to practise selfless loving as they turn and open their hearts to God. The purpose of prayer is to help a person to keep on loving, to keep on turning to the only One who can bring their imperfect loving to perfection. The important thing to remember is that there is no magic formula, no infallible method or technique. There are just hundreds of different ways of praying in order to do one and the same thing.

A means of prayer is good for you if it helps you here and now to keep gently turning your heart back to God. What may help you at the beginning of your spiritual journey may be of no use later on. What helps you in the morning may not help you in the evening. What helps you one minute may not help you the next. So move from one method to another with complete freedom.

Remember that these methods are only means to an end.

It is a good idea to be on one's guard against the 'here today and gone tomorrow' gurus, who have a fetish about a particular means of prayer which they impose upon everyone without question as the means to end all others. These people know nothing about the spiritual life. If they did they would know that methods of prayer change as people change, and as prayer develops with the years.

If you can find a good spiritual director or guide to help you, that is fine. If not, remember once again, there is no perfect means of prayer, just different ways to help you to do the 'one thing necessary', to love God with your whole heart and your whole mind and your whole soul. Any method of prayer that helps you do this is good; good for you, even if it does not help anyone else.

Chapter 34

Up with the violin, down with the kneeler

I had one of those out of body experiences one Sunday afternoon not long ago, shortly after the radio program, Gardeners' Question Time. I heard a strange rustling sound around my head, as if it were the flapping of angelic wings or the rustling of heavenly skirts. Then there was a blinding white light and the sound of heavenly music. The first thought that flashed into my head was, "I don't deserve it, I've done nothing to merit being here." My second thoughts were, "But where exactly am I?"

Then as I began to surface from my Sunday siesta I realised just where I was and what had been happening. The strange rustlings had come from the newspaper slowly slipping from my face. It had been filtering the pale autumn sunlight into a strange white light. The heavenly music was coming from the television. It was a concert to celebrate the ninetieth birthday of the London Symphony Orchestra.

The brilliant young Korean violinist, Sarah Chang, was playing Sarasate's Carmen Fantasy and it really was out of this world. Some have acclaimed her as the greatest violinist since Paganini, and she was then barely in her teens. She played in concert at the age of three and could sightread virtually anything at the age of eight. However it was not just her fiendish virtuosity that transported me, but the quality of her musicianship that had an other-worldly quality about it that even I could appreciate. She sent shivers down my spine and brought goose pimples up all over my body. I know you will think I am an old fool, but I ended up hunting for my violin that has been hibernating in the loft for many more winters than I can remember. I made a confounded nuisance of myself all evening scraping and scratching my way on to everyone's nerve ends.

When I woke up next day with painful arthritic fingers I remembered that my first music teacher said to me, "I'm going to free your hand through discipline, free you to play whatever you like whenever you like." I am afraid she never succeeded, but she did succeed in teaching me that true freedom always comes through discipline.

What is true of learning the violin is true of learning anything else. I am only free to drive the car wherever and whenever I choose because I subjected myself to the discipline demanded of me by my driving instructor. And what is true of every human accomplishment is especially true of the most important accomplishment of all – loving. I may want to be free to love everyone I meet, whenever I meet them, as Christ did, but I will never be able to do it unless I practise selfless loving at particular times set aside for that purpose.

Sarah Chang was gifted from the beginning with musical genius but she is the first to admit that only endless practice has enabled her to share her gift with others on the concert platform. She is free to play whatever she chooses whenever she chooses only because she has subjected herself to the daily practice she needed. Without that practice her unique gift would remain permanently dormant. It is exactly the same with us. Unless we freely subject ourselves to the necessary discipline of daily practice then the gift of God's genius that baptism bestowed on us will remain forever dormant too. It is only by practising loving as best we can that the gift of divine loving gradually suffuses our human loving, bringing it to perfection.

Prayer is the word Christian tradition uses to describe the time and place that a person sets aside to practise this loving. The more regular and the more intensive this practise is then the quicker we learn the most important of all human accomplishments.

The great Christian geniuses whom we call saints only became free to love whomsoever they met, whenever they met them, because they subjected themselves to the discipline of practising loving in prayer. The more they practised the more the divine love that has already been embodied in Jesus became embodied in them, and in their loving too.

Listening to Sarah Chang made me realise that I will never become a great musician no matter how hard I practise because I do not have the gift that she has been given. But it has made me realise that I have another gift that is even more valuable than hers and that can make me into a selfless Christlike human being if only I am prepared to practise like her.

I have put my violin back in the loft now but I have brought down my prayer stool instead. If I want to be anything like the Man I've chosen to follow I have to practise more regularly the prayer that enabled him to become what he was and raised him up to become what he is now. That is the only 'out of body experience' that I really want!

Chapter 35

In vino veritas

I am not one of those people who can just sit down and start having profound thoughts. What insights I do have from time to time come at the oddest of moments and in some of the unlikeliest of places. Take that holiday on the canals, for instance. I took what I thought was a short cut down a backwater that became narrower and narrower, so that it became quite impossible to turn by the time I came to the first lock. When I discovered that I could not turn the handle to open the gates, my thoughts were a million miles from the spiritual life, and so was my language until my first mate came to the rescue with a pot of oil. As I turned the handle she poured oil on to the cogs that were congealed with rust. Gradually with my efforts and the facilitating power of the oil the gates opened wider and wider and water came gushing in.

I did not shout Eureka and do an Archimedes down the towpath. The insight came later after a pint of 'Bishop's Tipple' in the Dog and Duck. Even then I doubt if it would have dawned on me had it not been Pentecost and had I not spent the preceding week preparing for the feast by reading a book, On Nature and Grace. The writer said that at Pentecost we do not just celebrate a great mystery that happened many years ago in the past, but a mystery that continues to take place in the present. God's love has been poured out and is continually being poured out on all who are ready to receive it. It is always there, surrounding us like a vast reservoir of supernatural life but we can only receive it if we freely choose to turn and open ourselves to allow it in. I could follow that, but when he went on to explain in rather complex theological jargon that we cannot even turn to receive it unless he gives us the grace to do so, he lost me. It was then that thanks to the 'Bishop's Tipple' my mind suddenly became clearer as I remembered my encounter with that obstinate lock.

Now I understood what that writer meant. Try as I might I would never have moved that handle to allow the water in without the facilitating power of the oil. That is why oil is used in the sacraments as a symbol of the Holy Spirit, the power of God who enters into our puny human endeavour to enable us to do what would be quite impossible without him. As we make a genuine effort to turn our hearts, rusted with sin and selfishness, to allow the living waters of the Holy Spirit in to transform them, it is the oil of that same Holy Spirit who enables us to turn and to turn repeatedly to receive it.

When St Peter told his listeners that Jesus was no longer dead but alive with a new life that he was even now pouring down on all, they begged him to tell them what they had to do to receive it. The answer was clear and simple: turn your hearts and minds away from all that separates you from what Jesus is pouring out and open yourself to receive it. The word St Peter used was 'repent', which literally means to turn and open your mind and heart and your whole being to God.

In the scriptures there is no word for a person who has repented, but only for a person or group of persons who are in the process of repenting. It is a continuous, ongoing process that never ends in this life until we do. This is exactly what the call to repentance means in the gospels and the response that St Peter demanded of those who would receive what he had received. It means to turn and to turn unceasingly to receive what Jesus is continuously pouring out to the end of time.

This continuous turning process is hard for us because of the sin and selfishness that has congealed and rusted the muscles of our hearts and minds. It will only become easier as, through continual daily prayer, the oil of the Holy Spirit is allowed to seep in to free them so that they can be more fully open to receive what was poured out on the first Pentecost day and is still being poured out every day.

Thanks to that obstinate lock and a pint or two of 'Bishop's Tipple' I was able to understand something of the mystery of Pentecost that I have never understood so clearly before.

Chapter 36

Monastic medicine

The drug companies have never had it so good. They are churning out antidepressants at a breathtaking rate. Almost everyone you meet is either on them, has just come off them or is thinking of going on them.

People who are in work are pressed to work harder and longer, with the threat of the sack hanging over them, so they turn to antidepressants to cope with the tension. Those who are out of work feel worthless, unwanted, a burden to others, and so they turn to antidepressants to help them cope too. Once upon a time people had homes where they would get love, security, and the support to soldier on through difficult times, but fewer and fewer have this luxury. More often than not broken marriages and broken homes add to the malaise that is undermining the human spirit in Western society. The only people who seem to have secure jobs in this sad new world are counsellors, therapists, doctors and psychiatrists.

The first time depression was recognised in a Christian community was by the monks in the Egyptian desert. They called it acedia. They became disillusioned and dissatisfied, not just with life in general, but with religious life in particular, which seemed to have lost all meaning. Many coped with it by losing themselves in work, weaving baskets and making pottery for the markets in Alexandria, or working the land to grow food for themselves and their fellow monks.

At all costs they tried to avoid the solitude they had originally sought for fear of the inner blackness that threatened to overwhelm them. Others who felt that nothing was worthwhile any longer did nothing only to find that things became progressively worse, as the devil found work for idle hands. Monasticism may never have survived had it not been for the wisdom of the great Desert Fathers. Gradually they taught the younger monks the discipline involved in living a balanced lifestyle.

They insisted that there had to be a balance between time for work, time for prayer and time for rest and relaxation. The monks were not expected or even encouraged to pray all the time, any more than they were expected to work all the time. Each monk was expected to do seven hours of manual labour, work that would be sanctified by the prayer that both preceded and punctuated it. Then there would be time for rest and relaxation and perhaps the pursuit of a hobby or pastime that would help balance the day. As each day was balanced with time for rest and relaxation, each week would be balanced in the same way by resting on the day when the Lord's Resurrection was celebrated.

Now I am not trying to offer any simplistic solutions to the contemporary malaise but merely to suggest that there may be something we can learn from the Desert Fathers. Once depression had set in, the great spiritual fathers would do for the monks what the best counsellors and therapists do today. They had their primitive forms of medication too, though these were often highly dubious and could not be compared with what is available nowadays.

If we are suffering from depression we need to seek professional help, but there is also Someone else's help we should turn to through the same discipline of a balanced lifestyle that saved the monks from despair. We need time to turn to God in prayer each day. We need to review our working day to try to make sure it does not envelop the whole of our day so that we have no time left for rest and relaxation with those we love.

We need to stop from time to time to take a long, hard look at the kind of life we live and see if we can improve its quality by making it more balanced. It is so easy for the balance to become distorted by circumstances that seem to control our lives. It may need merely a minor adjustment, but it may require much more than that. We may need to make a radical change to the whole direction of our lives, the work we do and the homes we live in, in order to have the sort of lifestyle whose quality is not determined by the salary we earn.

The best way to keep depression at bay is by living balanced lives that enable us to be more available to God and to each other. But additionally, as the first monks discovered, this not only prevents depression but opens a person to the peace that surpasses all understanding and the joy beyond all telling. This is the gift that was promised to all who are first prepared to seek God and his kingdom, and to continue to seek it above all else.

Chapter 37

Mr Swingtime's special

The neighbours have cut out an island bed in their front lawn that is the envy of the neighbourhood. Although I do not begrudge them the welcome attention they have received, I am not particularly amused by the way their success has made our weed-ridden lawn look even more mangy than usual. Though we have had a wonderful show of daisies and dandelions this spring, nobody has even mentioned them. They have been too busy gawping at the expensive shrubs and flowers of our neighbours. I was convinced that they must have come into a nice little fortune until they assured us they had not. It seems they had discovered a small family business way off the beaten track which sold expensive-looking shrubs for at least half the price of the other garden centres.

When our neighbours promised to show us where it was if we stopped shaming them and dug out an island bed for ourselves to complement theirs, we agreed. After we stocked up the car with more than we could afford they drove us to Mr 'Swingtime', the local fuchsia specialist who lives in a small caravan next to his greenhouses. They are flanked by a most beautiful garden, presided over by a small wooden summer house.

"That is where me and me dog sit every evening," said Mr Swingtime, "with a tumbler or two of whisky and ginger wine." It was his paradise regained by the sweat of his brow and the fruit of a Scotsman's vine. It is what he lived for, worked for, and made him feel that life was not so bad after all. Who's to blame him? Not me, I've joined him in 'spirit' myself often enough and know just how he feels. It is a nice feeling for those who know how to drink in moderation.

Some of the greatest mystics must have enjoyed a nice drink in an evening from time to time because they used the feeling to describe what it is like to feel the presence of God at the outset of mystical prayer. It is almost the same sort of feeling you get after a glass or two of your favourite tipple, minus all the side effects that always spoil it for those who go a tumblerful too far, as some of us do from time to time.

Imagine the pleasant, warm feeling that makes you feel good, makes you feel that life is for living, makes you feel at one with the world and everyone in it. Then subtract the idiot behaviour when. You have had one too many, the symptoms of withdrawal that wake you up in the middle of the night and the splitting headache that pursues you into the middle of the next day. Then, they say, you will have some idea of what the first experience of God feels like to the mystic. But it will have taken many years of prayerful preparation to experience what deep down we all desire more than anything else.

I suppose that is why we turn so easily to alcohol when we feel low, tense, tired and in need of a quick pick-me-up. Deep down we would like the real thing but we never seem to have the time to search and find through prolonged periods of prayer what seems so easily accessible through alcohol. That is why the young sometimes turn to drugs, to find what their parents seek from their drug. Both are seeking instant mysticism, instant escape from pressures of work or from tiredness with life and with the world that seems to give none of the hope, the meaning, and the fullfilment that it appeared to give in the past.

Of course there is no harm in a drink or two. Good luck to Mr Swingtime, but when it becomes for the older generation what drugs have become for the young it is a sign that something is seriously wrong. When more and more people depend on instant artificial experiences with potentially lethal side effects for body and soul alike, it's a sign that we have been deeply deprived of what we really crave.

I am sorry if I am beginning to sound like a wet blanket but I have a bit of a hangover this morning. You see, it was hard work digging out that island bed in my front lawn. It took me most of the day to do it and the rest of the day to plant it out. As a result I was too tired to pray at the end of it. So I repositioned my armchair to enable me to survey the fruits of the hardest day's labour I can remember, then I poured myself a tumblerful too many of Mr Swingtime's special. It is not the first time I've chosen the shadow to the reality and I suppose it will not be the last, but it has made me realise yet again what I really want more than anything else and made me resolve once more to seek it.

Chapter 38

From Siberia with love

Towards the end of the Second World War two young Polish women were transported to Siberia. Anna, the elder of the two, had left three young children behind in the village that had been razed to the ground by the Red Army. Her husband was captured by the Gestapo at the outset of war and was sent to Belsen where he died. Maria was unmarried, an only child, who had to watch as both her parents were shot and tossed into a common burial pit. Then she was pushed into a cattle truck, along with Anna, bound for the labour camp where few survived.

They became close friends and shared a crude straw bed in a flimsy wooden hut that was no protection against the freezing winter. Every night they huddled together for warmth and every night Anna cried herself to sleep for the three children that she left behind, and the fourth she knew she was carrying. Maria cried too at first, but then she began to pray for her parents, and she prayed for herself too that she may be of some help to her friend who had a far greater burden to carry.

The morale in the camp was appalling. People lived more like animals than human beings, each grabbing for themselves, fighting for food and drink and endlessly squabbling over matters that would have been considered trivial elsewhere. Shortly after their arrival the rations were cut by half which inevitably meant that many would die. Despite the fact that Anna was pregnant she seemed to manage as well as the others, though that wasn't to say much, while Maria got worse and worse until she died shortly after Anna's baby was born.

It was several weeks after Maria's death that the truth came out. Her prayer had been answered. She was given the strength to share the greater part of her meagre rations with her friend, so that Anna's baby could have the chance to survive, at the risk of her own life. The effect of Maria's sacrifice had a dramatic effect on the other inmates. They were so deeply moved by such selfless love that they felt ashamed of the way they had been behaving to one another.

People suddenly began to behave a little more like human beings. The fighting over food and drink all but ceased, and the endless quarrels became the exception rather than the rule. From a rabble that had been behaving more like brute beasts than human beings, the semblance of a community began to emerge. At first it was quite spontaneous. Then as morale was restored, leaders were chosen and the discipline that they imposed was accepted by all.

A wooden cross was placed over Maria's grave and it was revered by all for what she did, not just for her friend but for the whole community, by reminding them of what they had all but forgotten. Many nominal Christians admitted later that they understood the meaning of the cross for the first time, because they saw for themselves its symbolism enacted before them. They saw genuine selfless love made flesh in a way they had never seen before. Everyone who survived that camp was convinced that their survival was due to a miracle of love that brought about a rebirth, a genuine resurrection in one of the last places on earth that you would have expected to find it.

It's the gospel story all over again, told to me by a young Polish nun over twenty years ago. Naturally she was too young to remember the terrible conditions inside that labour camp where she was born, but her mother told her the whole story before she died in 1964. Sister Maria had retained her Christian name when she entered religious life, to remind her of the loving self-sacrifice of her mother's closest friend.

She believed that the miracle of rebirth in the Church and in religious life can only be brought about by those who are prepared to open themselves to the love that she first received through the self-sacrifice of the godmother she had never seen. She explained how it would involve great suffering, as all the saints discovered to their cost and our gain. She quoted the words of Alexander Solzhenitsyn who also experienced a rebirth in a labour camp similar to the one in which she had been born. "I believe that the rebirth in faith will only come about through those who suffer most".

I have never forgotten Sister Maria's story, nor those words of Solzhenitsyn. They have often inspired me to pray for the grace to journey on, come what may, to learn the self-sacrificial love that alone will bring about the rebirth in faith that cannot come in any other way.

Chapter 39

Mary's Sacrifice

We were all shocked and bemused when my brother announced that he wanted to become a priest. But it was not just that he wanted to become a priest, he wanted to become a Cistercian priest. That meant that once he left home he would never return again.

Naturally my mother was totally bereft. She was proud that her son wanted to be a priest, but why, oh why, did he want to become a monk as well? She did not know what to do, but fortunately she did know who to turn to. She turned to Gus, a friend since her childhood. He himself had left home to become a priest and a monk and was at the time the Abbot of Belmont.

He explained to her that a mother only really fulfills and completes her motherhood when her love is so great that she allows her child both to choose and to follow his own vocation in life, whatever that may mean. He told her that this was the sacrifice that Mary had to make when she had to allow the son to whom she gave birth to go his own way and to respond to the vocation that he was called to. My mother felt much better after talking to Gus, or Abbot Williams as he was then. After all he was a priest and a monk himself, and so he was able to console and encourage her better than anyone else.

Although my brother had been accepted as a prospective monk at Mount St Bernard's, the Abbot asked him first to finish his studies in Paris where he was studying at the Sorbonne. Naturally he was delighted that he had been accepted, because he was afraid that his handicap might have prevented him from becoming a priest. One leg was shorter than the other as a result of contracting polio when he was six.

Unfortunately my brother had a terrible accident on the way to his final examinations. Partly because of the iron caliper on his leg, he slipped down the steps to the Metro, hit his head and was killed instantaneously. He was only twenty-two. I was seventeen at the time and was called out of the school study to be told of the tragedy. When I went home it was to find my mother all but inconsolable. She had already come to terms with the sacrifice that she was asked to make when he chose to become a monk, now she was asked to make another, more complete and final sacrifice that she never thought for a moment would ever be asked of her. Once again she turned to Gus for spiritual help.

The whole of Mary's life revolved around selflessly giving her all for the dear son she had borne. Everything had always been for him, and then she had to give up absolutely everything, even him. This was the most perfect and complete sacrifice any mother has had to make, and she made it standing there at the foot of the cross. My mother never forgot what Gus said to her. It did not take away all the pain but it did give meaning to it and made it bearable. What helped most was seeing that the sacrifice she had to make was exactly the same sacrifice that Mary had to make at Calvary.

There is only one true priest and that is Jesus Christ who made the most perfect sacrifice anyone can make, the sacrifice of themselves. We are priests to the degree in which we share in his priesthood. Throughout his life he offered himself unconditionally to his Father and to the people whom his Father had sent him to serve. We share in his priesthood when we too offer ourselves to the Father and to the same family of man that he came to serve. "But you are a chosen people, a royal priesthood" (1 Peter 2:9).

That is what my mother came to see and understand more clearly than anyone else I know, not just in the way she thought but in the way she acted. It was a lesson that she had to learn at the most painful moment of her life when she had to share in the sacrifice of Christ in exactly the same way as Mary. Lessons learnt in such moments are never forgotten. They indelibly stain the memory and determine the way you think and act for the rest of your life, for better or for worse. In my mother's case it was for better, as it had been for Mary. For both of them it meant that through their terrible ordeal their motherhood had somehow been refined and deepened, to the benefit of other children who looked to them for the motherly love that was always given without measure. I for one know this because I have experienced it for myself, and still do.

Chapter 40

A time to mourn, a time to cry

My mother's death happened so quickly and was so unexpected that I had difficulty coming to terms with it at the time. Everything seemed so unreal. I just did not feel anything. Jobs had to be done and I had to do them. Someone had died and I had to make all the practical arrangements. My relatives were there but they did not support me; I organised them. I heard them say all the things you would expect them to say, and I said all the things I was expected to say. It was as if I was acting a part, and I was conscious of it—but what else could I do?

When I was home again and returned to work I carried on as if nothing had happened. The workload had built up during my absence and it took me months to catch up. The sudden cancellation of a major conference gave me two weeks off. Although I did not realise it at the time, it gave me the space and time I needed to come to terms with my mother's death. It took me a week to slow down. In the second week I read and reread a pile of letters that my mother had sent me over the preceding years.

The past came flooding back—all she did for me, been to me, all the sacrifices she made for me. Suddenly something that had been hard within me softened and the feelings and emotions that had been securely locked away welled up and overwhelmed me. Tears began to roll down my cheeks. I not only came to terms with her death but I celebrated her life, and her continuing life and love that I knew would never leave me.

On the following Good Friday when I was dutifully listening to the reading of the passion, something inside me said. "You have come to terms with your mother's death, but have you come to terms with Christ's death?" In a flash I saw how cerebral my faith was. Here I was, reacting to Christ's death as coldly as I had reacted to my mother's death the year before. Once again there was the same feeling of unreality, as if I was play-acting; as if I was detached from something or from Someone that I should be deeply involved with.

Some truths are just too big, too awful, or too awesome for the mind and the emotions to cope with; they just do not react to them. That is one of the reasons why so many people never get beyond first beginnings with their prayer life. They can manage with the prayers they were taught as children; they can even make up their own, especially when they want something from

God but they cannot get any further. They may believe every article in the creed, but it does not really touch them deeply. God is far away in his heaven and the gospels are two thousand years past.

Two things are necessary for prayer to grow beyond the stage of set formulas and petitions to the stage when it becomes a personal encounter with the most lovable man ever to walk on this earth. The first thing is to find some space and time in which to stop being 'busy about many things' so there can be time to come to terms with Christ's death, and to celebrate his life and love, and his continuing life and love.

The second thing needed is to read and reread every word that has been written about him in the gospels and to read everything that he said, because what he said is addressed to us personally, just as every word in my mother's letters was addressed to me personally. These sacred words are precious so they should be read slowly and prayerfully as you would pore over poetry to penetrate its meaning and experience its impact. Gradually in time, and under the influence of the Holy Spirit, the faith that once seemed solely cerebral will deepen, as hearts and minds that were like stone before soften and become porous to receive and experience the love of Christ ever more deeply.

When this happens, the feelings and the emotions react as the whole personality begins to respond in a perfectly human way to the most perfect human being of all. Prayer begins to grow, to develop and deepen, as in any other loving relationship. It expresses itself in the language of love as it responds to the One who now seems to rise out of the sacred texts, out of history, and to enter into the heart and mind of the person who has persevered in prayer beyond first beginnings.

As love grows and deepens into union, words finally fade away as they give way to a profound and pregnant silence. Meditation gives way to contemplation—the still, silent, and loving gaze upon the One whose life we now celebrate within us because we have finally come to terms not only with his death, but with his Resurrection.

Chapter 41

Seize the moment

I have to admit to being crazy about my teenage pop idol. No, it was not Buddy Holly, or Elvis, or even one of the Beatles. It was an opera singer, Tito Gobbi. I waited for four hours in the pouring rain to get a ticket to listen to his concert at the Free Trade Hall in Manchester. It was out of this world. I can still see and hear him singing the Largo al Factotum as I write. It was magnificent. I went home on a high that was followed by a terrible low for the rest of the week as I realised I would probably never see or hear him again, at least not in the flesh.

The musical genius that entranced me on that evening was unfortunately limited by the body that contained it. That body was subject to the same laws of space and time that limited me, so even one repeat performance was quite out of the question, at least as far as I was concerned. It was not every day that a man of such stature graced the stage of a provincial town.

It would have been the same if I had been alive at the time of Jesus. Opportunities to see him and listen to him would be strictly limited, because, like the musical genius of Tito Gobbi, the spirit of God's genius that was in him was limited by his physical body, by the laws of space and time that restrict everyone in the world into which he chose to come. It would be the same today if he was alive now as he had been then in the Holy Land. Seeing him would at best be a matter of coming and going, meeting, and departing, and that would be for the lucky ones. But the Resurrection changed everything. Jesus was swept up out of the space and time world that had restricted him before, only to re-enter it in a new way. This made him available not just to his disciples or the people of Israel or their contemporaries in the ancient world, but to all men and women in every part of the world and in every subsequent century simultaneously.

Tito Gobbi is dead now. I will never experience his musical genius again as I did before, but through the Resurrection Jesus is not only alive now but I can actually experience him, experience the spiritual genius that was his, coming to me from the inside through love. And I do not have to travel anywhere to be exposed to this love, nor do I have to wait for the right time for an appointment. The right time is now in this present moment. This is why the eminent French spiritual director de Cassaude spoke about what he called the 'sacrament of the present moment' because it is only in this moment that we can be open to the eternal life that Christ entered into on the first

Easter day, so that he can be available to all who would receive him every day.

The past is gone; it is over, it is finished. If what has happened in our past has to be redeemed in any way it can only be redeemed now, in the present moment. The future will never come to us except in the present moment, so we must get used to praying, with the popular hymn, "Lord, for tomorrow and its needs I do not pray ..." and learn to live in the present moment.

Even today de Cassaude's secular compatriots speak about the importance of what they call Le moment as the only time and place that is open to them to live life to the full. Old fools live in the past, young fools live in the future; those who freely choose to be fools for Christ's sake learn to live in the present because it is the only place that they can encounter him and the fullness of life he said he came to bring.

This is why the quality of a person's faith will not be determined by a comprehensive knowledge of past events in our Christian heritage, nor by an understanding of the complex explanations that are used to interpret them. It will be determined by the serious way in which we endeavour to open ourselves to receive the fullness of the Christ-life that is always ready to transform us now in the sacrament of the present moment.

Chapter 42

Living in the Present Moment

I was incensed when a foreign commentator said that the English are not really interested in tennis, they are just mad on Wimbledon. But when I thought about it I had to admit there was more than a grain of truth in what she said. I could name at least half a dozen people who plan their holidays to coincide with Wimbledon fortnight. Even if they never go in person, they spend hours glued to the television until the players with the fastest serve batter their way to victory on the final day.

I used to do the same myself but when the power players took over from the touch players my interest began to wane. I still watch from time to time, but I'm far choosier these days. In one recent year, I started to watch, but threw in the towel when Agassi was out, and did not even bother to watch the final on the Sunday. But I watched the women's final on the Saturday. At best, what the women lack in power and speed they more than make up for in finesse. Their rallies are longer and more exciting, and it does not all depend on the speed of the serve.

I always find that Wimbledon is something of a spiritual experience. Of course I do not watch for that reason, I watch because I enjoy the matches, or at least some of them, but every year the dedication of the players to what matters most to them makes me compare unfavourably my own dedication to what matters most to me.

It is the quality of their single-mindedness that always impresses me. When they set foot on the court it is as if they enter into a time-free zone where they are able to put everything out of their minds in such a way that they can live fully in the present. The past no longer exists, the future has no more meaning than the next ball they are about to hit. If they allow anything from the past to disrupt their concentration, even if it's a point that has been wrongly called against them or a piece of gamesmanship by their opponent, then it is instantly dismissed. Nor must anything from the future disturb them either. Just a few moments indulgence imagining themselves holding the trophy aloft or celebrating with their friends as they approach match point could mean that they lose it along with the championship that they thought was theirs for the taking. At the highest level in every sport the match is ultimately won in the mind.

I remember the Australian Lew Hoad being interviewed a year after his retirement from competitive tennis. He said that what he missed even more than the glory of winning, or the glamour of being a celebrity, was the 'high' he experienced when playing, as he lost himself in the joy of living more fully in the present than at any other moment of his life.

It is reminiscent of the spiritual theme that is usually associated with the writings of Brother Lawrence and de Cassaude, but it is a theme common to all the saints, who gradually discover for themselves that they can only be fully alive in the present moment. It is the only moment when time touches eternity and they can encounter the One who dwells there. God cannot be encountered in the past or in the future, but just in the present moment.

In order to live fully in this present moment, unencumbered by a past or a future that could destroy their 'naked intent' upon God, the first monks sought out a spiritual father to help them. In a practice that foreshadowed private confession and the psychiatrist's couch, they openly confessed the sinfullness and the guilt that indebted them to the past and prevented them from living fully in the present. Then they freely admitted their unruly and unbridled desires that did the same by making them live in the future.

Abbot Jacob used to say that past failings can be redeemed only in the present, where future failings can alone be prevented. When the past and the future no longer impinge on the present then the sort of singlemindedness that can be seen each year at Wimbledon can become the purity of heart that enables a person to see and experience the One who can be encountered only in the present moment and nowhere else.

I have to admit that that Foreign commentator was right after all, because I do not really care much about tennis or follow the fortunes of the players when the curtain falls on Wimbledon, until it rises again the following year. But the spiritual truths that I am reminded of each year do remain with me and help to impress on me what I should be doing all the time to live more fully in the present moment.

Chapter 43

Hacking into heaven

I happened to be passing through one of my pious phases when the vocations exhibition hit town. I was mesmerised by the spiritual goodies on offer. There was so much to choose from that I did not know where to start. How was I to know whether to hitch my wagon to this order rather than the next one?

Everyone gave me the same answer. "What a waste of time and money," I thought, to put on such a huge religious extravaganza to tempt people to join one order or another when God had already decided for you. I already received similar answers at school when I asked priests about other possible vocations in life, so I could not be blamed for having rather strange ideas about the will of God.

I came to believe that God must have some sort of vast filing cabinet in heaven in which his will for each one of us was filed away, charting every step we ought to take, from the cradle to the grave. The only way, therefore, to find out what God had already decided for us was to pray, so that we could in some mysterious way be given access to the contents of our personal file.

It was several years later when I was having second thoughts about the vocation that I thought God had chosen for me that I approached Father Germaine, my spiritual director. I realised then I had been wrong. "God's will is that you choose," were the words he kept repeating over and over again. "That is why he has given you a mind to think with and a will with which to choose."

"Well, why are we continually told to pray in order to find out what his will is?" I asked.

"Because prayer gradually purifies the mind and the heart so that the sin and the selfishness that always cloud our vision are gradually dispelled. Then we can see what we ought to do more clearly, and where we should be going with ever greater clarity. Prayer is not some sort of supernatural way of hacking into the celestial computer, or seeking illumination from the divine operator, it is a way of allowing the Holy Spirit to clarify and purify our minds and hearts. However, minds and hearts do not work in a vacuum so at the same time as praying they must be directed to searching for God's will in the scripture, in the teaching and tradition of the Church, and in how it is embodied in our own unique personalities.

"To do this successfully we need to consult others wiser then ourselves who know more about the scriptures than we do, more about the way they have been understood in the Christian tradition to which we belong, whether this means consulting them personally, or through their books or both. It means turning to someone else too, who can see us more objectively than we see ourselves. Then when we have done all these things and come to a decision that we act upon, we can be sure that we have done God's will, because God's will is that we choose.

"If, five years later, we look back and see that our decision may have been wrong, or could have been better, it does not mean that we did not do God's will at the time, because we most certainly did. Once again God's will is that we choose, to the best of our ability, in the circumstances in which we find ourselves, and with the best knowledge we have to hand at the time."

Thanks to Father Germaine my understanding of how to discover God's will was totally changed. Naturally I was asking him to help me at a particularly difficult crossroads in my life and so a lot of thought and prayer had to be put into it. However, in our day-to-day lives we have to make a thousand and one small decisions, but we can still be sure that we are doing God's will if we make them to the best of our ability and with the best will in the world.

But the more we raise our hearts and minds to God in prayer, the more God can cast away the last vestiges of sin and selfishness so that we can begin to see and act more and more like the perfect man, Jesus Christ. This is how, from doing God's will to the best of our ability, we gradually come to do his will to the best of his ability by doing it as Jesus did. Prayer not only enables us to see how to behave more and more perfectly, it gives us the power to do it, so that gradually our will and the will of God become as one, as they were in Jesus Christ.

Chapter 44

Hobson's choice?

Alec Cobbe was not a high-flyer except in his imagination. But unfortunately for him his intellectual powers were insufficient to raise him to the heights where he wished to shine. He had to be content, therefore, with a second-class degree at a third-rate university. However, after only ten years of teaching at a rather mediocre comprehensive school he managed to secure the post of deputy head in a secondary modern school by a combination of luck, well-placed friends and the ambition that never ceased to exhaust his imagination.

A timely death enabled him to be appointed as headteacher before the governors discovered that there was no more substance behind his confident smile than behind that of the Cheshire Cat. The school quickly became an extension of his own irrepressible ego that had to prove itself second to none.

Although his son had passed the eleven plus he had no choice but to join his father's little empire along with his younger sister, who did not even share the academic mediocrity of her father. They would prove to any doubters that his secondary modern was as good as any of the major comprehensives over which he would far rather have presided.

After years of intensive work the daughter managed to get four O levels and one low-grade A level, but sadly collapsed under pressure in her second year at teacher training college. She had a breakdown from which she never fully recovered. The son had all the intellectual powers that his father could have wished for himself, but none of his ambition. The father made up for the deficiency by willing him all the way to

Oxford, but there the son rebelled against the pressure to live out the ambitions of the man he had come to despise. He became a drop-out, a drug addict and a disgrace to his father. The mother finally left her husband to look after her daughter and to make a home to which the prodigal could one day return, God willing.

But God is not always willing to subject himself to human ambitions, nor to be determined by their consequences, nor is he willing to force his own ambitions on others. Like any father worthy of the name, he wanted true happiness for his own Son more than anything else – the happiness of experiencing the fullness of life that filled him, so that he could then share it with others. But nevertheless, he did not want to determine anything, so he gave his Son a mind to think with and a will with which to choose, so that he could 'grow in wisdom and understanding with the years' by using both of them.

One of the most difficult things that any parent has to do is to allow their children to grow up by making choices for themselves even when those choices differ from the parents' own. True fatherhood and true motherhood are brought to completion only by allowing one's children to choose their own way in life, though this may seem heartbreaking at the time. It is a most heinous form of immaturity to try to live out one's own frustrated ambitions through one's children and it can have devastating consequences.

No such immaturity exists in the Perfect Father whose will is that we choose for ourselves. Even though he knows that what he has to give, answers the deepest need in all of us, we must choose for ourselves. He forces nothing. Love cannot be forced on anyone against their will. Nor does he try to determine the context in which we should choose to receive it, or the way in which we should be continually open to it.

Though the language of popular piety may suggest otherwise, God's will is that we choose by using the mind he has given us for that purpose. Why else would he give it? 'Damascus Road experiences' do happen, but they are not the rule, nor are they primarily given for the personal wellbeing of the receiver, but for the wider community whom God chooses to reach out to through the individual.

Alec Cobbe thought he had something of a 'Damascus Road experience' when a set of fortuitous circumstances raised him to the head teachership of a suburban secondary school. He thought he was called to reshape the educational establishment with his revolutionary ideas that he sought to prove at the expense of his own family. I would love to be able to tell you that his story had a happy ending when he saw the error of his ways, but he did not. He ended his days in unhappy retirement, separated from the family he used to fulfil his own ambitions and from the God who he thought would have endorsed them. Like the school over which he presided, God was for him no more than a means of achieving his own overriding ambition.

Chapter 45

The Alien Corn

The BBC produced a brilliant play in the 1970s based on a short story by Somerset Maugham. It was called The Alien Corn and told the story of the eldest son of a Jewish family in Edwardian England. His father had made a fortune for himself, bought a large estate, become a member of parliament, and finally earned a title that enabled him to ease his way into society.

The play opens with an almighty row between the father the son. The father wants the son to go to Oxford and then return home to take over the estate, stand for parliament, and eventually inherit the title. The son refuses. He is dedicated to the arts; he lives for his music and above all he wants to become a world-famous concert pianist. Neither will give way and the quarrel seems to be getting out of hand when the wily old grandmother steps between her son and her grandson with a compromise that they both accept.

She says that if the grandson has not just great talent but real genius, then nobody, not even his father, has the right to deprive the world of what is a divine gift. Genius is never given to a person purely for their personal pleasure, but for the community with whom they have the privilege of sharing it. The agreement is that the young man will study at the Conservatoire in Munich for two years, after which he will return home to celebrate his twenty-first birthday, according to the wishes of his parents. Then, two days later he will play for the whole family and for one other, a world-famous pianist of his choosing, whose decision all will abide by.

When the big day comes, and the young man has finished his recital, the pianist he admires more than any other goes over to him, takes his hands in hers and asks what he wants of her. "Can I become a great concert pianist like you?" he asks. "You have played well," she replies. "You have studied well. You have mastered your technique and you will give great pleasure to yourself and to others, but a great concert pianist you will never be. I'm so sorry, but I'm afraid you lack the one thing necessary; it is the gift of genius. Only this gift will enable you to become what you desire to be more than anything else. It's a gift that you cannot acquire for yourself no matter how much you practise, no matter how hard you work to attain it."

The young man left the drawing room utterly dejected while the whole family congratulated the maestro on her decision, and themselves on their victory. The play ends with the sound of a single gunshot from the armory.

Genius is a rare gift and is given to an individual not for themselves but for others. It was the one thing that the young man desired above everything else so that even the gift of life itself had no meaning without it.

The poet Francis Thompson said that every Christian is given the gift of genius, not musical genius, or any other particular kind of genius, but God's own genius – the Holy Spirit, who is implanted from the beginning like a seed deep down within. If the right environment is created and all the obstacles to its growth are removed then that seed will invariably grow until it transforms its bearer into a perfect human embodiment of the One who planted it there in the first place. A saint is a person who has allowed this gift, which is given to all, to grow and grow until it attains its full potential in the human personality. Every single person who has received this gift is called to the heights of sanctity.

It is no good saying, "Well, that sounds all very well, but it is not for me. I am not called to perfection, to sanctity. I am just an ordinary run-of-the-mill Christian." That is blasphemy against the God who has destined all to reflect on earth something of the glory that is his in heaven. He did not make a few spiritual aristocrats, whom we call saints, and then make the rest of us commoners. That is what we may like to believe because it absolves us from the effort that is demanded of us.

The truth of the matter is that every one of us is called to the heights of sanctity by God himself, and we will arrive there if only we do our part so that he can do his. Our part is to create the environment and remove the obstacles so that the seed of his genius can grow and extend to every part of us.

Prayer is the environment, sincere sorrow and forgiveness will remove the obstacles:

that is our part, that will always induce God to do his. We may never become great pianists, great musicians, or great artists, but we can all become great human beings, if the seed of God's genius is allowed full scope in our weakness. Then we will see for ourselves, and so will others, what St Irenaeus meant when he said, "The greatest glory to God on earth is man fully alive."

Chapter 46

St David of Didsbury

Of course I had heard of St Francis before, but I was quite unprepared for the effect that Assisi had on me after ten days of sightseeing in Rome. Naturally I was impressed by the grandeur of the 'eternal city' rising majestically above the dirty streets, but after only half an hour I would have chosen Assisi every time. I was a bit cynical when I heard all the talk about the atmosphere of the place, about the aura of peace that was said to hover over the town, and the spirit of the saint that seemed to haunt it, but it was all true.

I never did work out whether it was the spirit of the saint that lingered on, or the charm of the medieval Umbrian town that seduced me but seduce me it did.

My seduction took the form of a search for all things Franciscan—in the school library, at the local friary, and from the old Franciscan, Fr Dominic, whom I sought out for confession whenever I found the opportunity. I was so impressed by the Franciscan saints I was reading that I decided to become one myself and asked the old priest to show me how.

"How can I become like St Francis, or St Antony, or like St Bernadine?" I asked him.

"Well," said Fr Dominic, "I have news for you. God does not actually want another St Francis of Assisi or another St Antony of Padua, or another St Bernadine of Siena, for that matter, but I'll tell you what he does want—he wants a St David of Didsbury! He's never had one of them before - how about it?"

God has made each of us totally different, utterly unique, so that every human being can reflect something of himself, of his goodness, his truth, his beauty in a completely different and unrepeatable way. He does not want us to try to copy someone else and become a caricature of them. He wants us to become ourselves. No one else can do what we can do. No one else can reflect on earth something of what God is in heaven in quite the same way as we can, if only we let him in to do in the end what he has always wanted to do in us from the beginning.

I know it is said that people are the same the world over and it is true that self-centred people are the same the world over: they are all turned in on themselves like soulless seeds. Most seeds look the same as each other until they are planted in good soil and given the light and heat they need, then they grow into something totally different as they flower into their true splendour and give glory to their Creator in unique and unrepeatable ways.

It is the same with human beings. Give them the right environment, open them to the light and the heat of love unlimited and they all grow into their true selves, and in becoming their true selves they all become totally different. Love makes everybody different, different expressions of the same love that makes three utterly distinct persons in the One God.

If you want to see just how different each seed can become when it receives all that it needs, you need to see it in full flower. It is exactly the same with human beings. Look at the saints: they are not all the same the world over, they are all quite different. Compare St Thomas Aquinas with the Cure d'Ars, St Augustine with St Francis, St Bernadette with St Catherine of Siena, or St Teresa of Avila with St Thérèse of Lisieux. You will see how they are all totally different. It was a song that I heard on the radio one day that reminded me of what

Fr Dominic said to me all those years ago. It was called, 'There'll never be another you'. It made me reflect on what had happened in the intervening years and made me realise how far I still had to go to become the man I was meant to be.

I know I will never become venerable or blessed, let alone a St David, but I do hope I will become a little more myself than I have been in the past. God wants everyone to embody and express on earth something of the glory that is his in heaven in as many different ways as possible so that the world may see, and in seeing may learn to believe.

Chapter 47

A very unlikely superstar

The first time I took part in a broadcast Mass was at the Grail in north London. Although the Catholic radio and television station was only just around the corner, Fr McEnroe, the producer, arrived only a few minutes before we were 'on air'. After apologising for being late he said it did not really matter too much because he knew we had practised the hymns and prayers that were to be recited together. But what really mattered was that we did not try to put on a show to impress the listeners. Once the rehearsals were over, he insisted that the most important thing we had to do was to forget that the Mass was being broadcast and to remember to pray as sincerely as we could – in short, to be ourselves.

A few years later I decided to enrol on a communications course at the National Catholic radio and television centre in London, where I eventually became the Dean of Studies. The one thing that has remained with me is the absolute importance of being yourself. You can fool some of the people some of the time, but you cannot fool all of the people all of the time. If you try to put on an act, to copy the broadcaster whom you admire most, or pretend to be someone other than you are, you will inevitably fail. You will come over as a phony, a hypocrite, a caricature.

We were told that the first television superstar was a rather portly middle-aged man with a small moustache and thick horn-rimmed spectacles. He was short-tempered, cantankerous and a bit of a bully towards the fools he was never prepared to suffer gladly. His name was Gilbert Harding. He became the biggest name in television precisely because he did not try to impress, to show off or be anything other than the man who was exactly the same on or off screen.

Each morning before the classes began, the Dean of Studies led morning prayer and gave us pep talks that supplemented what we learned from the tutors. He said we did not just have to be ourselves as we are, but something of ourselves as God wants us to be, so that what we said could be heard and seen embodied in what we were. Mother Teresa, Archbishop Anthony Bloom and Pope John XXIII were given as perfect examples of effective Christian communicators. They were not effective because they had received the sort of knowledge that we were being given, but because they received the sort of knowledge that God gives through prolonged prayer. They became their true selves, the selves that God had destined them to become because they were open to a far more profound knowledge than anything that the BBC presenters and producers who came to speak to us could ever hope to impart. It is this knowledge that can enable us to see ourselves as we are and then give us the strength to become what God has destined us to become.

Many years before I learned from my spiritual director that God's will was that we should choose. Now I found what he wishes us to choose more than anything else. He wants us to choose to become our true selves. After all, that is what he created us for, or he would not have created us at all. He wants us to choose to receive the true wisdom which is love, so that we can receive the inner help and strength to become our true selves, in the same way that Jesus chose and became his true self.

Gilbert Harding was no plaster-cast saint, that is for sure, but most people admired and even loved him because he had the courage to be himself when so many people do not. He did not like what he was or the way he sometimes behaved, as he admitted later in his life, but his honesty and integrity opened him to receive a grace that changed his life. He saw what God really wanted of him, who God wanted him to become, so he joined the Catholic Church and began to seek the help and strength he needed. He became a far mellower and a far more compassionate man before he died, much closer to the man God wanted him to become. He will not be canonised, but that is not the point. The point is that it was his honesty that opened him to the grace we all need if we are going to become anything like the person God wants us to be.

It is a long journey, a lifetime's journey, but it is the only journey that is really worth taking. It is not just for ourselves but for others too, who seeing, may be inspired to follow, as Gilbert Harding inspired me.

Chapter 48

If only the canon hadn't gone off

If I had to choose eight comedy videos to take to my desert island Absolutely Fabulous and Fawlty Towers would top the list, and if I had to choose only one it would be "Fawlty Towers". So you can imagine my delight when I heard that Jennifer Saunders and John Cleese were on the BBC's program, 'Desert Island Discs' during the Christmas season.

Though neither of them would nail their profession of faith to the door of any particular church, it was clear that they both believed in a spiritual dimension to their lives. Jennifer Saunders said she felt like rushing out to get baptised every time she heard the Bach B Minor Mass, though she never did. The spiritual dimension was evidently important to John Cleese too, though he did not feel any of the organised religions knew anything about it.

Interestingly enough, I had just been reading the results of a survey presided over by David Hey, formerly of the Alistair Hardy Research Centre at Oxford. Amongst other findings he discovered that sixty per cent of the general population of this country admitted to having a personal spirituality that influences their lives, though less than ten per cent of the population are regular churchgoers. It would seem that if these surveys come at least somewhere near to the truth, they represent both a criticism and a challenge to those of us who are insiders, belonging to the sort of organised religions with which my favourite comedians feel they cannot identify.

A highly intelligent and articulate friend of mine, who would identify with John Cleese, divided contemporary Christians into two groups – the emotional extroverts and the emotional introverts. The first group, he says, puts you off with their effusive evangelical fervour that tends to be naive and fundamentalist. The second group puts you off with their low-key 'take it or leave it' approach. and they do not go out of their way to help you, or to help you understand what evidently seems to mean something to them.

I took my friend to Mass with me some months ago hoping that the power of the divine would somehow get through to him despite the frailty of the human. Unfortunately the frailty of the human was even frailer than usual that particular Sunday. The canon who is usually so good was away, and his substitute gabbled through the Mass at a breathtaking rate of knots. The sermon was so full of jargon that even I could not understand it, and the priest left the altar like a whirlwind so that the altar boys sprawled on the floor in his wake, tripping over their cassocks trying to keep up with him. Then to top it all the congregation suddenly lapsed into loud and seemingly inconsequential chatter that might have advanced the social well-being of the community but did little to give the impression that they realised the awesome significance of what they had just celebrated. I was mortified.

"Does that priest and his congregation believe in the meaning of the Mass as you explained it to me?" my friend said as we got into the car.

"Yes, of course," I said. "Well, they could have fooled me," he said, "but they didn't." We drove on in silence. There is something wrong, deeply wrong, about the way we both practise and communicate what we believe to others. I know I keep beating the same drum, for which I make no apology, but I know no other. It is the same drum that every serious searcher has beaten since Christ rose from the dead. His continual presence amongst us is experienced only by the poor and humble of heart who know how to receive and savour that presence.

Prayer is merely the word that is repeatedly used in the Christian tradition to describe how this receiving and savouring is done, and how the recipient is changed in the receiving. Had the canon been there that Sunday I feel that something might have been different. Like the parish priest who presided when I was a boy, he is always there before you, preparing for what is evidently the most important event of his life. I know it is not his Mass, it is our Mass, but he presides over it and unless he in some way embodies the One he makes present to be embodied in us, something vital is missing in the celebration.

John Cleese might not have been converted had he come to the canon's mass, but at least he would not have been able to say that they know nothing about the spiritual. And who knows, Jennifer Saunders might well have been baptised after all.

Chapter 49

What we want is more prisms!

While pursuing further studies in Rome my parish priest went to San Giovanni Rotundo in southern Italy, where he stayed in the Capuchin friary where Padre Pio lived for most of his life. He not only saw for himself how the padre prepared for his morning Mass, and how long he prayed after it, but became aware of the powerful effect that it had on his life, and on the lives of those who came to receive from him something they could not receive from anyone else.

The priest told me how the pilgrims, who came from all over the world, would fight to get the best places in the church to see the man they believed to be a living saint. No actor had such a presence, nor such an effect on those who came to see him, yet it was obvious that the padre was totally oblivious of the effect he had on everyone. He seemed to be lost in another world that absorbed all his attention. Without realising it, he communicated something of the mysterious holiness of that other world to everyone present in such a way that their attention was wholly drawn towards him, and through him, into the mystery that he was celebrating.

When Padre Pio made his way back to the sacristy my parish priest looked at his watch and was astonished that he was there for over an hour, yet it seemed no more than a matter of moments. The spirit of silence, the sense of reverence that had been totally absent at the beginning of the Mass, now enveloped everyone. Those who made their way out of the church did so as if in a daze. It was as if they had been sedated by the same spirit of holiness that enveloped the man who presided at the altar. The Mass itself had not changed, it was the same Mass they had attended many times before, but never before had they received its fruits in such a tangible way.

The man who represented Christ at this celebration was so open to him that he not only embodied him in a unique way, but he was also able to communicate what he had received to others. It was as if his physical body had been transformed into a spiritual prism that first received and then transmitted to those present something of the limitless power and energy that was unleashed in the sacred mystery over which he had presided. What those present had experienced made them want to change their lives irrevocably for the better. It made them want to seek forgiveness for their failures in the confessional, where the man who had drawn them there read their souls like a book and read them with an understanding and compassion that they had never known before.

His experience at San Giovanni Rotundo taught my parish priest more about the liturgy that he was studying in Rome than all the lectures he attended put together, at least in what really matters. It gave him a true perspective that is so easily forgotten by liturgists who are all too often preoccupied with externals that express their own personal aesthetic preferences or individual theological orientations. The sacred liturgy that finds its fullest possible expression in the Mass has one aim and purpose that comes before all others. That is to draw all who participate into the mystery of Christ, to share in the life he received in its fullness so that they can live and love as he did. Then he can continue to make his presence felt in the world he came to serve through them. All signs and symbols, whether they find their expression in words, in music or in sacred rites or rituals, are employed to this end.

But what my parish priest learned in San Giovanni Rotundo was that the most important sign of all is the person who represents Christ himself at the altar. Even if all else fails, if he genuinely embodies the person he is privileged to make present on that altar, then the effect will be incalculable. To this end my priest never spent less than half an hour preparing to celebrate the sacred mysteries, and as long, if not longer, afterwards relishing what he had received.

I may never have had the good fortune to be present at Padre Pio's Mass, but I have had the good fortune to be present at numerous Masses celebrated by my parish priest many years ago. He is dead now but his example lives on for me, and for many others, who but for him would never have understood or appreciated what is the most powerful force for good in the world.

Chapter 50

Back to the future

I always fancied myself as a speaker because I considered I had a good voice, or a 'big mouth' as my friends put it. So you can imagine my delight when I went to my first lecture in what in those days was called 'sacred eloquence'. The lecturer gave a brilliant analysis of the problems of the world into which we would soon be sent. "The gospel," he told us, "has all the answers." His job was to teach us to communicate those answers to the world that would be lost without them.

I knew he had missed the point. I was reading a book at the time called The Resurrection by F. X. Durwell. This explained how the gospel is not primarily a body of truths, but a Body full of love that was raised from the tomb on the first Easter day. It argued that the Apostles were witnesses to the Resurrection, not just because they had seen that Body, but because they too were filled with the same Spirit that made it radioactive with the love of God.

That is why the first Apostles achieved so much in such a short time. People listened to them because they saw something of the One the Apostles spoke about actually embodied in them before they even opened their mouths. There is all the difference in the world between a good preacher—someone who has a fine voice, a gift of words and an ability to engage their audience—and an effective preacher who moves their audience, not so much by what they say or how they say it, but by what they are.

The Curé d'Ars was not a good preacher in the sense that he had a fine voice, a gift of words or extraordinary communication skills, but he was an effective preacher because of what, or rather who, he was. His sermons read like an anthology of pious clichés. They would leave you cold, but they left his congregations white hot, burning with the same Spirit who was literally embodied in him.

My grandmother told me of an old lady in her parish at the beginning of the century, who heard the Curé speak when she, as a young woman, was on the 'grand tour'. His sermon changed her life though she did not understand a word of it! The Curé had been sent to the parish at Ars because it was of so little consequence that his superiors thought he could not really do any harm there. Even those who spoke up for him had to admit that he had no more than average intelligence if that. The majority thought he was a dope who should never have been ordained.

Nor did he have any illusions about his own ability. That is why he did what arrogant people never do. He turned to God to do for him, and through him, what he could not do for himself. Night after night he spent in prayer, preparing for what he knew he could not do without it. This is where he received the same Spirit that filled the first Apostles, that enabled him to do in his small parish what they did before him.

Towards the end of his life some forty thousand people a week came to listen to him, from all over Europe and beyond. The man the church authorities had originally thought too dumb to become a parish priest spoke more powerfully than any other and did more for his parish than any of his contemporaries. That is why he was not only canonised but held up as the patron saint of all parish priests, the model above all others for them to follow if they would aspire to embody the Spirit as he did.

If we still want a dynamic 'decade of evangelism' which was declared in the 1990s, in which to transform the world, then we must learn from the Apostles and precede it with a decade of retreat, in which to practise the personal prayer that will enable the Holy Spirit to do in us what was first done in them. The Curé did not spend weeks or months, but years in prayer, for hours each day, to receive in ever fuller measure what he could then give to others.

Perhaps parish priests could give us all the lead, by doing themselves what their patron saint did before them. You do not need to have all the eloquence of men and angels or know all the mysteries there are, but you do need the love without which we are no more than gongs booming or cymbals clashing. That love is always given to those who humbly seek it in prayer. What we have to give most of all is not clever answers to problems, but the love that is the answer to everyone's deepest problem. It might have been a good idea to finish this 'decade of evangelism' where we should have started in the first place, by trying to receive for ourselves before we presume to give to others. Until we go back to basics we cannot go into the future with anything more than empty words.

Chapter 51

A drop in the ocean

I remember attending a frightening mission in our parish when frightening missions were still in vogue. It all began with a solemn procession from the back of the church, led by the missioner carrying a large crucifix on his back. When he reached the front, he mounted the pulpit, raised the cross for all to see, and shouted as loud as he could, "That is what your sins have done to Our Blessed Lord."

The thought appalled me. I had not really given it much thought before but I did then and I found I simply could not believe it. It made no sense. I could willingly admit that I would have played the coward with the Apostles, even denied Jesus as Peter had done in the heat of the moment, but by no stretch of the imagination could I see myself scourging him, crowning him with thorns, or hammering in the nails. My spiritual director sympathised with my feelings but he did not take away the responsibility for the sufferings of Christ, he relocated it.

"No," he said. "We are not personally responsible for the sufferings of Christ in the first century, but we do have a responsibility for the sufferings of Christ in the twenty-first century." We have a responsibility now for the Christ who suffers again and again in our day from the same evil that nailed him to the cross in his day. Jesus made it quite plain on numerous occasions that it is he who suffers in the neighbour in need, and it is we who are called upon to help him.

This responsibility is not an optional extra, it is placed on all of us. Jesus made it clear that the question that will be asked of us when the final day of reckoning comes will be, "Did you serve me in the neighbour in need?" The final judgement upon which our eternal future will depend will not be assessed by how many miracles we worked, how many people we healed or how many ecstasies we had, but on how we responded to Christ who continually suffers in the suffering of our fellow human beings.

One of our problems today is that we are continually bombarded, particularly on the television, by the needs of our neighbours from all over the world and we just do not know where to start, who to turn to, how to begin: the task seems so immense, the needs so great. I remember a particularly cocky television interviewer pressing Mother Teresa of Calcutta about the nature and scope of her work. Finally he said to her, "But after all, is what you are doing but a drop in the ocean?" She smiled and said very simply, "Yes, but is the ocean not made up of many drops?" We cannot do everything, we cannot even do very much, but we can do something. Too often it is our arrogance that lets us down. We have to think that our 'great acts of charity' will change the world, or at least make a major quantifiable contribution that will be noticed.

In medieval Europe there was a mystique surrounding the service of the deprived that was embodied in story after story about the lives of the saints. It all began with that famous episode in the life of St Martin of Tours before his conversion. He was approached one freezing cold day in deep midwinter by a beggar who was half naked. Martin had nothing to give so he took out his sword and cut his cloak in half so that he could share it with the poor man. Later he learned that the poor man was Christ.

Such stories abound throughout the literature of the Middle Ages. Almost all of them convey something more: they show that the givers themselves receive in the act of giving. St Martin is converted by his encounter with Jesus in the beggar in need. St Francis is transformed by kissing the leper he found so repulsive the moment before. I remember being bored on a pilgrimage to Lourdes, so I started to look after the sick for the sake of something to do. I received so much that it turned out to be the most rewarding experience of my life.

It is in giving that we receive. This is one of the great secrets of the spiritual life that is learned by those who hear the cry of Christ rising from the needy. They discover that in trying to meet the needs of others it is they themselves who receive in return far more than they intended to give. The promise made in the gospel is quite clear. All who seek and serve Christ in the sufferings of the neighbour in need will be sought and served by him in the life of love without measure.

Chapter 52

A new beginning

There was a special moment of solitude that I always used to relish before the day broke and fragmented itself into little pieces. It was a moment when some of my more bizarre inspirations surfaced from the subconscious. I think it had something to do with the harvesting of the morning's stubble that reminded me of my responsibility to make constructive contributions to the well-being of homo sapiens. And so it happened that particular new year's eve.

My morning ritual was interrupted by one of my fellow students reciting one of the more popular poems of his compatriot Robbie Burns in his annual bath. "Yes," I thought, "The bard was right. If we could only see ourselves as others see us!" I took his words as a text with which to preface a spontaneous little homily to my fellow students during the coffee break in the common room. The point with which I ended was that instead of making our own new year's resolutions we should make them for each other.

The lack of enthusiasm that greeted my inspiration had ill prepared me for the deluge of brown envelopes that I picked up at my door with such pleasure the following morning. If I had sown in tears I had certainly reaped in joy. However, what I thought was a great triumph turned into a humiliating disaster, as I read one resolution after another made for me by my fellow students.

"Why not resolve to mind your own business in future?" "Stop trying to organise other people's lives until you've learned to organise your own." "Keep your facile inspirations to yourself, you supercilious hypocrite." And so they went on in similar vein, all twenty-three of them. Naturally I have had to translate their language into the repeatable. Students have their own way of expressing their feelings that is not always acceptable to the wider community.

What I thought would have been a triumph turned out to be a humiliating disaster, but thanks to Kipling I learned to 'treat those two imposters just the same'. I had long ago learned to trust myself when all men doubted me, so I thought I would retire and live a more eremitical lifestyle, only helping those who learned to trust me as I trusted myself. I had forgotten what Kipling said about making allowance for your own self-doubts, because I did not have any - at least not until the bottom fell out of my spiritual life!

It began when all feeling and all fervour seemed to evaporate overnight. It was as if God had turned his back on me to talk to someone of more importance. As the weeks and the months passed by I began to wonder whether or not he would be returning, and when he did not, I began to wonder whether he was there at all. Then, as I began to lose all confidence in him, I began to lose all confidence in myself, who believed in him for so long. Suddenly my spiritual life collapsed, leaving me in a black hole from which I could not seem to escape, try as I may.

At first I became angry at the so-called God of love who did this to me if he existed at all. I became sour, sarcastic, and cynical, and projected the bile that was in me on to those around me, but nothing helped - nothing changed. In the end I was forced to reflect on my past because I did not seem to have any future, forced to come face to face with what I was before. My fellow students were right, I had been a self-righteous prig. I had been a supercilious hypocrite and I still would be it were not for the black hole from which I could not escape.

When you are in one of those black holes and you begin to see yourself for the first time as others see you, you know for sure that you cannot even help yourself, never mind others. If this leads you to turn to God for help as never before, you come to see in time, in God's time, not yours, that black holes can be full of grace when their occupants are full of humility. That is what they are there for. I made a resolution there and then never to make resolutions for other people, whether they are new year's resolutions or any sort of resolutions for that matter. When you have glimpsed in some small way, something of yourself as others see you, it makes you realise you have more than enough on your plate trying to keep your own resolutions, never mind making them for others.

So I won't end this book by suggesting resolutions that you could make, but by making one for myself: No more books until I've at least tried to put into practice for myself what I have had the cheek to write about for others!

www.ingramcontent.com/pod-product-compliance
Lightning Source LLC
Chambersburg PA
CBHW020639230426
43665CB00008B/232